Socrates on Judaism, Christianity, and Islam

Socrates on Judaism, Christianity, and Islam

Asking the Right God-Questions

Doug Van Scyoc

Resource *Publications*

An imprint of *Wipf and Stock Publishers*
199 West 8th Avenue • Eugene OR 97401

SOCRATES ON JUDAISM, CHRISTIANITY, AND ISLAM
Asking the Right God-Questions

ISBN 13: 978-1-59752-865-8

Manufactured in the U.S.A.

Dedication

Jana Renee Ota Van Scyoc
April 9, 1982—March 19, 2005

Contents

Preface

IS RELIGION true? Does God exist? What happens to us when we die? What should that mean for us while we are alive? Are these the greatest of all questions and, if so, why?

After thousands of years and countless religious traditions, why does the world continue to hunger for spiritual truth? Why are religious lives so often filled with doubt, worry, and dark nights of the soul? It has been said that if we don't challenge our beliefs, our beliefs will eventually challenge us.

Do you believe in pregnant virgins? Do you believe in the incarnation of an immutable God? Do you believe that an eternal God died? Do you believe that one God consists of three Gods (God the Father, God the Son, and God the Holy Spirit)? Do you believe a loving Jesus will return to bring the world to a tragic end? Do you believe that two contradictory notions cannot both be true?

We are defined by our beliefs. Dysfunctions stem from an erroneous view of the world and one's relation to it. Someone sitting on a completely unreasonable belief system is sitting on a time bomb. Voltaire said, "Those who can make you believe absurdities can make you commit atrocities." He was most likely referring to the horrors associated with Crusades, Inquisitions, witch hunts, and Reformations.

Can you prove what you believe? If you have proof, then you don't need to believe and you certainly don't need faith. Can stories prove anything or show us how to prove something? If you don't have proof, why do you believe something while knowing it cannot be proven? Beliefs that one cannot prove are often wrong. Our beliefs help to create the world in which our descendants will live. With that said, are we guilty of perpetuating a world of illusion?

The God question can never be solved. No one can prove that God exists and no one can prove that God does not exist. Absence of evidence, however, is not evidence of absence. All I know is that I don't know and that I can't know. What I do know, however, is that it is never a good idea to assign unobserved features to entities.

Jesus said that we shall know the truth. What is truth? Truth is an accurate description of reality. Truth never envelops itself in mystery. Truth never needs to be defended; it can stand on its own. Are truth and faith mutually exclusive?

We can never know if we have final truth. In a search for truth, you will only discover what is not true. Interestingly enough, what drives humanity forward is this quest for nonapparent truth. At the end of the day, the only things we really have are potential truths. Nothing in life or death is guaranteed.

That's the bad news. The good news is that humans can discover that their core conceptions are false and replace them with truer ones. The search for truth can free you from the myths that bind you. It's about the journey, the seeking, and not about the elusive destination. The journey of controlling belief by fact begins with a basic understanding of world history, mythology, religion, philosophy, and science.

Do you believe the human anatomy is designed for meditation or mobility? Let's not go there.

Acknowledgments

I would like to acknowledge the God or God gene that forced me down this perilous path and enabled me to survive it. I would also like to thank my managing editor, Jim Tedrick, and my copy editor, Carrie Wolcott, for making this book possible.

Introduction

GLOBAL CRISES and disillusionment with religion are forcing believers to question the basis of their faith. Millions of Jews, Christians, and Muslims are currently struggling with the confusion and doubt that continues to plague their various traditions. *Socrates on Judaism, Christianity, and Islam* was written for those who are not satisfied with the belief system they encountered in orthodox religion.

This book is a spiritual and intellectual journey through world history, mythology, religion, philosophy, and science as it pertains to Judaism, Christianity, and Islam. More importantly, it is a brutally honest and extensive search for God.

The Holy Bible, history, and mythology are used extensively to scrutinize the truth claims of Judaism, Christianity, and Islam, and to determine if a reconceptualization is required for each of the faiths. Using the Socratic method, I ask soul-searching questions that academics, clergy, and reflective laypersons think about but seldom address. I dissect each faith—looking closely at origins and cultural expressions, exploring piece by piece, examining major doctrines and stories—to ask what makes sense and what doesn't make sense, what is functional and what is dysfunctional, what works and what doesn't work in today's world.

Living in doubt with an illusion is hell, whereas living in harmony with the truth is liberating. The startling discoveries revealed in this book promise to eliminate much of the uncertainty that plagues those who hold to Judaism, Christianity, and Islam. My hope is that this book will assist others as they embark on their solitary quest for spiritual discovery.

CHAPTER I

Seeking God in Truth

A N ANCIENT skull from a remote monastery mocks me. It says, "I was once like you—soon, you will be like me." The face of death haunts me in the winter of my life; hearing its footsteps compels me to seek God. Pursuing the divine, somehow, brings peace of mind.

I'm being facetious. The truth is that my sugar-coated Christian world was shattered years ago when I heard a Holocaust survivor and Nobel Laureate say, "All the killers were Christians" and "Hate is a Christian problem." Shocked and deeply offended, I spent the next several years researching Christian history only to find the supreme Christian value of love literally drowning in a pool of blood. Millions of men, women, and children had been slaughtered by those baptized in the name of Jesus Christ. It hurt to hear people say that they didn't think the world could bear another two thousand years of "Christian love."

For whatever reason, there seemed to be a serious disconnection between the "good news" of the Christian gospel and the catastrophic events that accompanied it. A Native American Indian once said, "When the white men first came, we had the land and they had the Bible; now, they have the land and we have the Bible." Was it ever really about God and love, or has it always been about land and economic calculations?

I tried to find encouragement in the sacred Scriptures—the source of divine inspiration. What I discovered instead was the God of Israel commanding the Israelites to exterminate men, women, children, and infants (1 Sam 15:3). Isaiah 34:6 reminds us that "the sword of the LORD is bathed in blood." In modern-day Israel, I listened intently as a Jewish woman referenced the Hebrew Bible to justify the displacement of Palestinian Arabs. She claimed that God had given his holy people all the land.

Is the God of the universe a real estate deity who favors some of the world's children while rejecting others? The reality is that Jerusalem, God's city, is a place cursed by religious enmity, and the Holy Land continues to be a region where one hates one's fellow human to the greater glory of God. Will their refusal to love their neighbor continue to kill them, and us, forever?

The holiness of Israel has been characterized by its separateness from other peoples. The stress on exclusion and concern with difference persists today. Many white militia movements also embrace this exclusive concept of religious or racial purity. The more identity people have, the more likely they are to hate their neighbors. Jesus taught us to love our neighbors, and even our enemies, because he knew that the truly sacred does not divide. The sooner humanity wakes up to this fact, the better.

The sorrow of the universe is ignorance. Ignorance stems from our constant susceptibility to deception, our passive acceptance of beliefs, and our conditioned existence. Suffering, more often than not, is the result of our ignorance. The song of the universe is truth. But what is truth in a world where nothing is what it seems? The sun appears to rise and fall and yet, in reality, it is a fixed star. At the end of the day, the fatherhood of God has not produced the brotherhood of man.

Thanks to the media, the image of a person holding an AK-47 rifle in one hand and the Qur'an in the other has been etched in the popular imagination. What we in the West fail to understand is that the vast majority of Muslims perceives Christianity as a religion in competition with Islam and that Western values are recognized as a threat to Islamic society. Many Christians also perceive Islam, the fastest growing religion in the world today, as a threat to global salvation. There can be no doubt that the point of contact between the Christian message and the Islamic world is a head-on collision.

Despite such issues as the Christian Crusades and Islamic terrorism, Muslim-Christian relations have not always been negative. Akbar the Great, a Muslim ruler, left a powerful epitaph at the Gates of Victory:

> Jesus, peace be upon him, said this, "The world is a bridge—cross it, but build no house upon it. The world endures for but an hour—spend it in devotion. The rest is unseen."

Losing My Religion to Find God?

To believe or not to believe?—that is the question. I've often wondered: did I abandon God or did he abandon me? What does it mean to have a religious or mystical experience? For that matter, what does it mean to have a déjà vu experience? While reading the New Testament late one evening in the spring of 2002, a Spirit touched my soul in a way that radically transformed my life. It was that unsolicited and mystifying experience that launched my relentless quest for the divine.

Did Jesus reveal that another God existed who had never been mentioned in the Holy Bible? Before he left the world, Jesus said, "I am returning to my Father and your Father, to my God and your God" (John 20:17). Jesus had a God? Can a God have a God in monotheism? Am I worshiping God in truth if I am worshiping Jesus instead of Jesus's God?

Jesus depicted a compassionate God who is loving, forgiving, and merciful. Is there a deity beyond what some scholars refer to as the brutal, partial, and murderous God of sacred Scripture? If there is, I had to find him. But isn't the quest for God the biggest wild goose chase in history? Why did Jesus say, "Seek God's kingdom and righteousness" (Matt 6:33) instead of "Go to church and read the Bible"?

Unfortunately, exclusive claims and defense mechanisms inherent in organized religion and various sacred texts ensure that truth is always easier to know than to seek. Does the solitary quest for spiritual discovery threaten religious institutional control? Is the shield of faith for the vast majority simply the will to avoid knowing the truth?

Does faith allow one to believe in spite of overwhelming contradictions, absurdities, and doubts? Is *faith* just another word for false hopes and beliefs? Why do some people accuse the faithful of ignoring all the hatred, slaughter, intellectual oppression, and viciousness of the Bible and its God? Is there a strong tendency among believers to close their minds to every fact that does not suit their personal prejudices or spiritual indoctrination?

It is human nature to cling to beliefs that offer the most comfort and security. Religious convictions, however, can be extremely dangerous. The blind leading the blind in unadulterated fanaticism have left millions dead in their wake. Wrong beliefs have led human beings to create a world of turmoil, suffering, and tragedy. There are those (Christians) who place their faith in a human sacrifice and there are those (Muslims) who sacrifice themselves for virgins in paradise. Sacrifice is a primitive rite of sacred destruction prevalent in virtually every religious tradition. Wasn't it God who said, "I desire mercy not sacrifice" (Hosea 6:6)?

Will you remain in a state of passive dependence, or can you handle the truth? An honest and extensive search for God is akin to a prolonged chipping away of the soul. It has been said that the finest steel is forged in the fieriest furnace. Living in harmony with the truth is liberating, whereas living in doubt with an illusion is hell.

There are at least three prerequisites for seeking God in truth. First, you must be able to free your mind from all fixed conceptions. Second, you must be willing to overcome ignorance in order to awaken to truth. Third, you must have the fortitude to continue the quest for there is much to bear and the road can be treacherous.

To coast through life in ignorance, ignoring ultimate questions, is to miss the whole point of being alive. It makes sense to ensure that our beliefs are as true as they can be. Often, however, we are incapable of recognizing the twisted state of our view of reality.

The myths that bind us most are those we do not perceive. How can we be certain that our convictions are not mere delusions? Intellectual and spiritual darkness stems from ignorance and religious indoctrination. Ironically, numerous personal truths are inevitably exposed as personal ignorance in an in-depth probe for God.

Beginning at the End: Apocalyptic and Messianic Expectations?

In Judeo-Christianity, an initial search for God usually begins with the Holy Bible. At the end of such a quest, one is forced to ask a very difficult question: Is the biblical God a reneger? In other words, how does a person who believes in the literal truth of the Bible reconcile the God of Noah—who promised that he would never again doom the earth or annihilate all living things—with the apocalyptic God of Daniel or Revelation—who wills a final genocide and the violent end of the world?

Why didn't God tell Noah that at the end of time he was really planning to wreak havoc on all but a few faithful Christians? The greatest story ever told begins with a global genocidal flood and ends with a terrible destruction of the earth and a ravaging of humanity. If the biblical God is love, where is the love?

After more than two thousand years, the human fascination—more often an obsession—with the end times continues. The book of Revelation, the last and most dangerous book of the Bible, remains a powerful force today. One Christian cult society, with over six million members, spends an inordinate amount of time each year peddling its interpretation of these dark prophecies door to door. The authors of the *Left Behind* series have sold more than 60 million copies of their work.

Apocalyptic imagery has captured the imagination of tens of millions of people, some of whom have followed its prophecies to tragic end. Apocalyptic prophecy has been linked to the recent fire that engulfed the Branch Davidians and to the conflagration that destroyed ancient Rome in AD 64. Some scholars believe that there was an early Christian summons to turn prophecy into reality by setting fire to the evil Roman capital and burning it to a cinder. Did the Roman emperor Nero persecute Christians throughout the empire because of their insurgency in Rome?

Bible-code research and analysis is now being used—in addition to apocalyptic literature, sermons, and door-to-door sales—to fuel the ongoing belief that we are indeed living in the end times and that the book of Revelation is going to be fulfilled, quite literally, in our lifetime. Millions of Christians are fearful that their nonbelieving friends and loved ones will soon be "left behind." Are these fears rational? What does it mean to live a life in fear of Armageddon and hell? What happens to people who spend their lives spinning in the neurosis of sin and salvation?

Modern scholarship suggests that the book of Revelation is not a prophecy about the end of the world but merely an attack on ancient Rome and an interpretation of the book of Daniel. The book of Daniel was directed against Greek oppression of the Jewish people while the book of Revelation was aimed at Roman domination.

Biblical scholars point out that the "Four Horsemen of the Apocalypse"—the Bible's most terrifying figures and the ones responsible for the ravaging of humanity—first appear in the book of Zechariah. Scholars also agree that the Jewish writer Enoch borrowed images from Greek mythology. These images resonated through apocalyptic literature down to the book of Revelation (e.g., Revelation 20:1–3 says, "The head angel who rebels against God is thrown down to earth in a pit called Hades."). The concept of angels, devils, heaven, and hell and the dream of victory in the war between God and Satan are also Greek in origin. Did John, the mysterious author of Revelation, simply copy and modify the Old Testament text for the first century?

It was customary for pre-Christian Roman emperors to be declared gods and worshipped after their death; they also had temples and cults dedicated to them. Was Revelation merely an urgent message or warning for a tiny minority of first-century Christians in danger of being seduced by the rampant paganism of emperor worship? Is the worship of the *beast* symbolic of the worship of the Roman emperor? Was the message designed to scare insiders into staying on the straight and narrow path? Were the visions less about predicting the future and more about chastising those who joined the cult of the divine emperor?

Megiddo, the bloodiest place in ancient Palestine, is believed to be the battlefield of Armageddon and the setting for end of the world. Rome's Sixth Legion, infamous for brutalizing its victims and striking terror throughout the empire, was stationed at Megiddo. Was Armageddon simply another image meant to evoke hatred for the Romans?

Does the *whore of Babylon* in Revelation symbolize Rome—the evil empire? Some scholars believe that the satanic *beast* or *antichrist* referred to the Roman emperor and that *666*, the devil's number, represents the emperor Nero (*616* corresponded to Caligula). While Nero persecuted the early Christian community, Caligula ordered a statue of himself to be placed inside the temple in Jerusalem, a sanctuary reserved for Israel's one true God.

Modern scholarship also suggests that the biblical concept of apocalypse may have originated in the teachings of the Persian prophet Zoroaster. The earliest apocalyptic belief is Zoroastrian. The understanding of life as a conflict between the forces of darkness and the forces of light is a Zoroastrian idea, which has come over into Judaism and Christianity. Several centuries before Jews and Christians made their predictions, Zoroaster predicted a final battle and a last judgment between good and evil. He prophesied that at the end of time a Savior would come to earth to resurrect the dead, reward the good, and punish the wicked.

In Hinduism, the *Gita's* story is set in the dramatic context of a war in which the good side is destined to overcome the evil forces. A war scroll found among the Dead Sea Scrolls also tells of an inevitable clash between the sons of light and the satanic sons of darkness. We know that the book of Revelation foretells one final battle between good and evil at Armageddon; this will be the flashpoint signaling the end of the world.

Across the Atlantic, in a region known today as Mexico, the Aztecs performed human sacrifice on a vast scale to appease their gods. According to their tradition, only human blood and hearts could satisfy the gods. Several thousands of victims were butchered each year because the Aztecs believed that without this daily sustenance, the gods would not permit their world to continue. In Hinduism, the role of Brahma is to create the universe, that of Vishnu to preserve it, and that of Shiva (Siva) to destroy it.

It is fascinating that Hindus, Zoroastrians, Jews, Christians, Muslims, and Aztecs—all from distinct cultures—entertained similar notions of apocalyptic myth. Does this give us some insight into the human psyche's ability to create fatalistic superstition?

The author of Revelation—like John the Baptist, Jesus, and Paul—believed that he was living in the climactic moments of history and that things were about to happen soon; but of course, they never did. Many scholars agree that John the Baptist and Jesus were apocalyptic prophets who proclaimed that the kingdom of God—the end of normal time and the beginning of a reign of goodness and peace—was at hand. They also claimed that the day of judgment was coming and called for a return to a pure nation of Israel.

The Apostle Paul was extremely apocalyptic. He relied heavily on apocalyptic language and themes to explain Jesus's crucifixion. Paul also believed that Jesus's second coming was imminent and Paul probably never expected to die before the kingdom arrived. The early church was convinced that the end would come within a generation; but like its leaders, it too would be disappointed.

Many people consider the book of Revelation an immoral reading. Some ancient Christians were appalled by Revelation and tried to ban it from the Bible because it conflicted with Jesus's message of love. The theme of Revelation is violence against one's enemy, whereas Jesus taught that one should love his enemy. Many early Christians also believed that the final battle was already over because, through Jesus's death and resurrection, love had conquered evil.

The church faced an interesting dilemma in the fourth century: Rome, the *whore of Babylon,* suddenly and unexpectedly became Christian under the emperor Constantine. As the new center of church power, Rome could not be *Babylon*; therefore, the apocalyptic reading had to be wrong. Christians didn't know what to do with the book of Revelation.

The Eastern Orthodox Church decided to exclude the book of Revelation from its version of the Bible. Martin Luther, on the other hand, would later use it to identify the pope as the antichrist. Satan in the church meant that the world was soon coming to an end. Everyone seemed to have an apocalyptic vision, which they applied to everything. Adolph Hitler also used apocalyptic language to label the Jews as the antichrist; he claimed that they would devour the people of the earth.

In the final analysis, was the author of Revelation really presenting us with a literal or unique vision of the end, or was his aim simply to attack the Roman Empire using contemporary events and ancient apocalyptic tradition? Is the significance of Revelation to be found in the past and not in the future? If we accept the fact that God is not a reneger and that Revelation is "history," must we also acknowledge the improbability of a second coming of Christ?

Many scholars agree that Jesus did not specifically speak about his own second coming. It is believed that Jesus's return to earth to judge both the living and the dead, as depicted in the New Testament, is a concept borrowed from Zoroastrianism. Is Jesus's future coming a myth? Is it possible to reconcile the Jesus who preached nonviolence, forgiveness, and love with the violent, apocalyptic, and vengeful God of Revelation who would appear on the clouds of heaven and bring the world to an end?

Is it imperative for Christians to rethink the eschatological aspect of their faith? Is there a real danger in second-guessing God and in claiming to decide what he can and cannot do?

In Mark, the earliest Christian gospel, God clearly states that Jesus is his Son. But in the last book of the Bible, we discover Jesus proclaiming that he is "the Alpha and the Omega"—the Lord God. Recognizing that one had to choose between Christ and Caesar, did the early Christians elevate Jesus to divine status in order to compete with Rome's new God—the emperor Augustus?

The Romans believed that Caesar was a god and savior who brought peace throughout the earth and whose divine birth was "good news" for the world. Did the Jesus movement adopt a similar theme in its development of Christianity? Is the Christian worship of Jesus a response to the pagan worship of Augustus? These puzzling questions prompt us to ask: is Jesus really the Messiah (Christ), the Son of God, and God?

The Israeli Disconnection?

Is Jesus the Christ, the Savior of Israel? According to Israel, he is not. The Israeli Supreme Court has ruled that Jews who believe in Jesus as the Messiah, or Christ, are not Jews. Is Jesus the Son of God? Not according to Judaism. Judaism believes that nobody could be the Son of God. For Israel, Jesus is neither the Messiah nor the Son of God. Israel's rejection of Jesus spans nearly two thousand years and now seems to be officially and permanently fixed.

Christian belief varies widely among its various branches. Its primary unifying principle is the belief that Jesus is the Christ—the Savior of Israel. Jesus said, "Whoever rejects the Son will not see life for God's wrath remains on him" (John 3:36). Salvation would come only through accepting Jesus as the Son of God.

According to Christian tradition, does Israel's rejection of Jesus as both the Messiah and the Son of God mean that Israel will neither see life nor receive salvation? Is Jesus truly Israel's Savior? If Jesus is not Israel's Savior, can he be the Christ? Can Christianity be a valid faith without a legitimate Christ?

God? Who's Who?

John the Baptist taught Jesus how to keep his identity a secret. What does it mean to describe oneself as simply "a voice crying in the wilderness"? The mystery of Jesus's identity fragmented Christianity into thousands of sects and cults and remains an ongoing topic of great debate. The confusion is understandable. Throughout the New Testament, *Father* is used interchangeably with *God*; the title *Lord,* a Jewish term for God, is used interchangeably with *the Son*; *the Son* is called *God* on numerous occasions. We also find Jesus claiming to be the Son of Man, the Messiah, the Son of God, and God.

The problem may be the simple fact that no one is listening to God. Who does God say Jesus is? In the Gospels, God specifically states that Jesus is his Son. God did not say, "Jesus is God," nor did he say, "Jesus is the Messiah" (or "the Christ"). According to some scholars, the title *Son of God* simply indicates that Jesus had a special relationship with God that had nothing to do with establishing divine nature. In the ancient world, "Sons of God" (Pharaoh, Alexander the Great, Caesar Augustus, Jesus of Nazareth, etc.), like miracle workers, were a dime a dozen.

In the Jewish tradition, *Son of God* is used to refer to angelic beings and spirit persons. Again, Judaism believes that nobody could actually be the Son of God. The Jews also did not conceive of the Messiah as divine. The first Christians were Jews who believed the Messiah had come. They also believed that Jesus was the Son of God who had risen from the dead after his crucifixion.

But who does Jesus say that he is? In Revelation 1:8, Jesus claims to be God—not the Son of God, but God Almighty. And yet, in Mark 13:32, we recall Jesus saying, "No one knows about that day or hour [of the end time], not even the angels in heaven, nor the Son, but only the Father." If Jesus is truly an immutable and omniscient God, why doesn't he know when Armageddon is supposed to begin? So whom should we believe: Jesus, God, or both? Are they really saying the same thing?

The Bible teaches us that there is only one God; that God is omnipotent, omniscient, omnipresent and eternal; and that God is both spirit and immutable (never changing or varying). Jesus is a God of Christianity. The foundation of Christianity is that Jesus is equal to God in every way.

If Jesus is equal to God, why does God refer to him as merely a servant in Isaiah 53? Why did Jesus say that the Father was greater than he in John 14:28? Jesus echoed the fact that the Father granted him authority to teach, perform miracles, and forgive sins. If Jesus is equal to God, why did he need authorization from God? Why did a coequal deity pray to another coequal deity? If Jesus is God, why was he praying and worshiping himself in solitude?

God is the powerful ruler of the universe. Pontius Pilate, a Roman prefect, was the powerful ruler of Jesus's universe. Is it possible for an immutable and omnipotent God, who walked on water and commanded the forces of nature, to become so weak that he is unable to carry his own wooden cross? If Jesus is truly an omniscient God, why did he cry out, "My God, my God, why have you forsaken me?" (Matt 27:46)? How does an omnipresent deity abandon another omnipresent deity? More importantly, how did an immutable and eternal God die?

The Bible informs us that after Jesus's death, bodily resurrection, and ascension, he "sat down at the right hand of God" (Mark 16:19). If Jesus is God, why did he sit to the right of God? God specifically states that he is immutable: "I the Lord do not change" (Mal 3:6). Jesus taught that God is spirit.

If God is both spirit and immutable, neither the assertion of the incarnation—that "God became man"—nor a bodily resurrection makes sense. God represents absolute perfection. The doctrine of incarnation contradicts the fact that an absolute being cannot change. To assert that God transformed himself from an infinite spiritual being to a finite physical being is akin to calling an immutable God a liar.

For many people, the notion of an eternal God visiting earth in the person of his Son merely to die for the sins of humanity is as mythical as the idea of a woman actually being the mother of God (the creator and sustainer of the universe). Hellenistic literature is full of miraculous births: Herakles, who was called Hercules by the Romans, was the son of Zeus (king of the gods) and Alkmene (a human consort). Herakles was the only human to be granted immortality among the gods. Ancient heroes, who were usually the offspring of a god and a woman, were worshipped as eternal spirits who could intercede on behalf of mortals.

The early Egyptians believed that Osiris was a king who came down from heaven and that Isis was impregnated by divine fire and bore a divine son. In Mithraism, a religion of ancient Persia, the god Mithras is born in human form and ascends to heaven. Krishna is the human-incarnate of the Hindu god Vishnu (a member of the Supreme Trinity); he resumed his divine nature after his death. The Buddha was an ever-existent eternal being who assumed human form. The Romans also believed that Caesar Augustus was conceived of a divine father and a human mother.

It is not surprising that the early Jewish-Christian community rejected the divine fathering and virgin birth of Jesus; for them, the stories sounded too much like pagan myth. For contemporary Christians, however, the incarnation stands as a unique, momentous, and decisive event in history. The incarnations of Osiris, Mithras, Krishna, the Buddha, and Caesar Augustus preceded the incarnation of Christ. Knowing this, can we honestly maintain the belief that the Christian doctrine of incarnation is truly unique?

In Greek mythology, we find stories about the messengers of the gods—those who carry the divine word to mortals. The ancient Greeks also believed the Oracle at Delphi spoke the word of God. The Christian belief is that God's eternal word became the word of God incarnate and then became the gospel. The New Testament, according to some scholars, never mentions the incarnation of God anywhere. John 1:1 states, "In the beginning was the Word, and the Word was with God, and the Word was God."

Of course that is not what is written in Genesis 1:1: "In the beginning God created the heavens and the earth." Why doesn't Genesis 1:1 mention anything about the word of God? The ancient Greeks wrote, "In the beginning, there was chaos!" According to Chinese tradition (the Chuang Tzu), "In the beginning, there was nonbeing, and nonbeing has no name." Why are there so many different "In the beginnings"?

The Mormon version of the Bible includes a passage in Genesis 50 that predicts the coming of Joseph Smith. In the Qur'an, Jesus foretells of Muhammad being his successor. Is it me or is there a noticeable trend here? Is it possible that Jesus is just a prophet in whom God worked rather than God incarnate? The incarnation—the possibility of an eternal being existing in time and then dying—poses an enigma, a rational incoherence.

When a wealthy man in Mark 10 addresses Jesus as "Good teacher," Jesus responds by saying, "Why do you call me good? No one is good but God alone." If Jesus is God, why does he repudiate the term *good* for himself and redirect it to God? Jesus often reminded his hearers that their highest obligation was to love God, not him, with the whole of their being.

Jesus taught his followers what we today call the Lord's Prayer (the Our Father); at no point in his ministry did he instruct them to worship him. Some scholars have stated that Peter and Paul never claimed that Jesus was God because the gospel that Jesus preached was not about himself but about the Father. Jesus was obedient to his Father's will; he spoke only what was given him to speak and did exactly the things he was commanded to do. He was all about his Father's business.

Was the Roman emperor Constantine responsible for officially elevating Jesus to divine status? The Roman senate usually voted on the deification of an emperor. Did the church bishops at the Council of Nicaea in AD 325, under pressure from Constantine, similarly vote in favor of Jesus's divinity?

Constantine attributed a stunning military victory to a miraculous vision from the Christian God. At the time, Christians were condemned to death throughout the Roman Empire. Constantine raised Christianity from a state of persecution to the empire's official religion. He replaced the Roman gods and adopted the cross as his victory symbol. It is interesting to note that in Roman myth deities appeared to men in visions or came to fight alongside them in battle. Castor and Pollux, the divine sons of Jupiter, were said to have intervened in the battle of Lake Regillus in 496 BCE.

It was the church Council of Nicaea that eliminated the subordination of Jesus to his Father by defining his divinity and emphasizing his equality with God. The council declared that Jesus and the Holy Spirit were one in being with the Father. The problem is that Jesus's obedience and subordination to God is upheld throughout the New Testament. Were the church's actions at Nicaea nonbiblical and in violation of God's first and second commandments? In their enthusiasm to create the Holy Trinity, did the church unwittingly produce another golden calf?

The New Testament was not defined until AD 367 and was not accepted in the churches until the fifth century. What this essentially means is that the Christian canon was formulated more than three hundred years after the time of Jesus and some forty years after the Council of Nicaea. Prior to the canonization of the New Testament, Christians considered the Old Testament their only Scripture.

In the New Testament, Jesus claims to be the Son of Man, the Messiah, the Son of God, and God. Because of the many different titles, some scholars believe that Jesus didn't claim any of them. Jesus was a humble man who was more interested in God and God's kingdom rather than in himself. Many biblical scholars also agree that Jesus did not elevate himself to the status of God. They argue that the first Christians accomplished that feat by making claims for him in their sacred writings.

Decades after the crucifixion, many Christian stories in the New Testament were created to fulfill ancient (messianic) prophecies in the Hebrew Bible and the needs of the early church. In the gospel of Mark, Jesus's life and actions are not set out as the fulfillment of Scripture, but they are in the latter gospels of Matthew and Luke. The New Testament authors went to great lengths to portray Jesus as both the Jewish Messiah (for Jews) and the Son of God (for Gentiles). In doing so, did they distort the historical Jesus?

For first-century Jews, the idea that their Messiah (military conqueror and deliverer) was crucified as a common criminal was completely unacceptable. The early Christians endured persecution from both Jewish and Roman authorities and suffered ridicule from their fellow Jews. As Christianity was forced to move beyond the borders of Israel, the concept of a Jewish Messiah would have been irrelevant in the various Gentile (non-Jewish) communities. The evangelists would have been compelled to say that Jesus was something more: *Son of God* was a title that Gentiles could relate to. To compete with Rome's new God, Caesar Augustus, it may have been necessary for the first Christians to elevate Jesus from "Messiah" to "Son of God" to "God."

Contemporary Christians will need to eventually grasp the truth that God is beyond Jesus. "This is what the Lord says—Israel's King and Redeemer, the Lord Almighty: I am the first and I am the last; apart from me there is no God." Isaiah 44:6 confirms that God is Israel's redeemer. Can the same be said of Jesus? Christianity began as a Jewish sect that believed that Jesus of Nazareth was the promised Messiah or Christ—the redeemer of Israel. But is Jesus truly Israel's redeemer?

Jesus clearly stated, "Whoever rejects the Son will not see life for God's wrath remains on him" and "No one comes to the Father except through me." Israel's rejection of Jesus makes their redemption impossible according to Christian tradition. If anything, the "Jesus event" drove a permanent wedge between God and Israel and created an alienation that cannot be reconciled. Because Israel has been alienated rather than redeemed, Jesus cannot be Israel's redeemer. God alone can bring redemption according to the Bible.

Can a similar argument be used to prove that Jesus is not the Christ? God promised the Jews that he would send a Messiah to deliver them. The exact identity of the Messiah was supposedly never given. Some biblical scholars, however, argue that Zerubbabel—the Persian-appointed governor and descendent of David—was the Messiah. The Old Testament prophets predicted that the Messiah—a Savior chosen by God—would deliver the Jews from foreign rule and restore the kingdom of Israel. The fact of the matter is that Jesus did not deliver the Jews from Roman rule nor did he restore the kingdom of Israel.

The Jewish prophets also believed that the Messiah would come from the house of King David. Despite the fact that Matthew and Luke tell two different and contradictory stories of Jesus's birth, they both agree that it is Joseph rather than Mary who is a descendent of David. This, however, presents some problems for those who insist both on Jesus's direct descent from David and on the doctrine of the virgin birth. The virgin birth—a common myth in Hinduism, Buddhism, and Zoroastrianism—contradicts belief in Jesus being the Messiah. These contradictions call into question the inerrancy of the Christian Bible and the claim that it is divinely inspired.

The bottom line is that the Anointed One must redeem God's chosen people (Israel) in order to fulfill messianic prophecy. According to Christian tradition, Israel's rejection of Jesus essentially means that it will be spending an eternity in hell. Because Israel has yet to be redeemed and because Jesus is truly not a descendent of David, he cannot be the Messiah, the Christ, or the Anointed One. Israel is still waiting for their Messiah. It is interesting to note that many distinguished biblical scholars have indicated that Jesus never claimed to be the Messiah. Is it possible then that there can be no Second Coming of Christ since the initial Messiah never really came?

The Messiah, according to the prophets, had the additional task of healing the wounded, giving life to the dead, and preaching "good news" to the poor. If these had been the only criteria for establishing the Messiah's identity, then there would be no doubt that Jesus was the Christ; but, unfortunately, they are not.

Were messianic expectations, like apocalyptic visions, merely created to give hope to a desperate people? Jews continue to wait for their Messiah, Christians continue to wait for the second coming of Christ, and Muslims continue to wait for their Hidden Imam. Are they all simply waiting for an illusion created by their religious ancestors?

Who Was Really Responsible for Jesus's Death?

The events leading to Jesus's crucifixion—and the blame for his death—have been the source of untold suffering and atrocity. After Mel Gibson's movie, *The Passion of the Christ*, was released, some churches immediately posted signs blaming the Jews for killing Jesus. But are the Jews or Jewish authorities really responsible for Jesus's demise?

Some scholars believe that Jesus's baptism by John convinced Jesus that he was indeed the promised Messiah. Jesus's teaching and healing ability drew and galvanized large crowds who also saw him as their long-awaited Messiah.

Jesus was a fierce critic of the Jewish temple system. He believed that the temple was no longer a holy place but a den of inequity and corruption. Priests lived lavishly, never mingled with common people, and manipulated Jewish purity laws to exclude undesirables. Jewish law precluded the lame, blind, sick, and deformed from gaining access to the temple. If you were sick, handicapped, or disabled, you deserved it—the wages for sin was death.

Jesus defied the Jewish establishment by healing these outcasts and instructing them to return to the temple. For one to three years, he traveled around the country and used the symbolic power of healings and parables to undermine the Jewish authorities. He would later do the same in Jerusalem.

In the Jewish tradition, only temple priests acting on behalf of God could forgive sinners. Jesus shocked everyone by forgiving the sins of a prostitute, healing a Roman centurion's servant, and welcoming Samaritans and Gentiles into the Jewish faith. In essence, he upstaged and bypassed the temple by healing the infirmed, forgiving sins, and presuming to speak for God.

The parable of the good Samaritan was designed to cast priests in a negative light and to break down social barriers. Loving your neighbor also meant loving your enemy. No leader or prophet in Jewish history had ever spoken in such terms. Jesus's radical teachings and actions made him both popular and dangerous. There is no doubt that he was seen as a threat to the Jewish establishment.

In first-century Judea, there was a heightened sense that the apocalypse was imminent. The Jewish people were expecting their Messiah to attack the Romans and reign in God's kingdom. The annual Passover festival in Jerusalem celebrated Jewish liberation from foreign domination and oppression. Anyone posing as a Messiah or doing "Messiah-like" things during this heightened period of religious tension could easily spark a rebellion. Two thousand men had been crucified after a rebel attack against the Romans. Rebels, "Messiahs," and fanatics were everywhere.

Jesus's timing was deliberate; the temple drew him like a moth to a flame. His kingly entrance into Jerusalem during Passover season was the prelude to his inevitable demise. He also did a number of things that were considered subversive and were certain to get him killed: (1) he undermined the symbolic basis of Rome's authority by pitting the kingdom of God against Caesar and claiming the God of Israel is the only legitimate king of the Jews; (2) he upstaged the temple establishment by criticizing the legalistic excesses of Judaic law; (3) he preached a baptism of repentance for the forgiveness of sins instead of sacrifice, the source of temple wealth and power; (4) he called for the religious renewal of Israel in God's name; (5) he overturned tables and threw out the moneychangers; and (6) he symbolically destroyed the temple by invoking the words of the prophet Jeremiah. In a prophetic act of negation, Jesus stated that the temple, made by human hands, would be destroyed. He believed that God would bring down the temple because it no longer practiced justice.

When Jesus, self-designated spokesman for God, preached in the temple, he was not only considered radical but deeply offensive. His insistence that he was the Son of God also drew fierce opposition and set the temple priests and leaders of the synagogues against him. Jesus's lifting of himself up to the level of God by claiming to be the Messiah or king of the Jews is probably what got him killed. The priests would have perceived the nature of his claims to be blasphemous whereas the Romans would have understood them to be subversive. Because he clashed with both Jewish and Roman authorities, and because he was considered a threat to the peace, stability, and welfare of the Jewish people, Caiaphas and Pilate decided that he had to be eliminated for the common good.

Threatening or disturbing the Pax Romana (the peace of Rome) usually incurred the wrath of Roman legions. Jesus was a popular prophet who had a substantial following. His reputation, teachings, and actions in the temple could have easily given the crowd of pilgrims the perception that he was indeed the promised Messiah. Jesus could have inadvertently sparked a revolt similar to those that eventually occurred in AD 70 and 135 in which hundreds of thousands of Jews were systematically slaughtered by the Romans.

According to biblical tradition, God repeatedly sent prophets to confront both political and religious establishments.

Jesus often quoted the prophets. He was well aware of the plight of the prophets of old and of the fate of John the Baptist in particular. He understood the consequences of confronting political and religious leaders in Jerusalem during Passover season. But Jesus also knew that more and more Jews were becoming increasingly destitute. The luxurious and excessive lifestyle of the wealthy priestly class may have infuriated him. There is no doubt that he was on a mission—responding to a prophetic call or personal vision—that compelled him to do what he did.

So who was ultimately responsible for Jesus's death? Neither the Jews, the Romans, nor God can be held accountable for Jesus's demise. Jesus bears sole responsibility for his death. He sacrificed himself in an attempt to help the Jewish people and reform his religion, which he believed was the will of his God. Jesus may have also believed that his sacrificial death would occur simultaneously with the end of the world in a single apocalyptic event.

Prior to Jesus's public demonstration in Jerusalem, John the Baptist had protested against the temple establishment by circumventing its sacrificial system and mediating God's forgiveness himself. The forgiving of sins was not unique to Jesus. John the Baptist, temple priests, and other religious communities also performed such rites. Baptism, the immersion in water, symbolized the forgiveness or remission of sins. Jewish law, however, clearly stipulated that only temple priests were allowed to perform sacrifices and mediate between God and humankind. These rituals were the source of great wealth and power.

Long before the crucifixion, both John the Baptist and Jesus had threatened the temple system by preaching a baptism of repentance for the forgiveness of sins and by calling for the religious renewal of Israel in God's name. In doing so, they collectively signed their death warrants. It was only a matter of time before one would lose his head and the other would be crucified. At the end of the day, Jesus's life seems to resemble that of a prophet rather than a Messiah, "for surely no prophet can die outside of Jerusalem" (Luke 13:33).

The Jesus movement, from beginning to end, was an anti-temple movement. The Jewish temple system had established an institutional monopoly on the forgiveness of sins and on access to God. Jesus, on the other hand, had offered an alternative path to God. By teaching his followers the Lord's Prayer, Jesus had shown them how to access God apart from convention, tradition, and institution.

After Jesus's death, his followers claimed that he was the Lamb of God who was sacrificed for sin once and for all. For Jewish Christians, this meant that temple sacrifice was no longer necessary. The early church also claimed that Jesus was the only way to God. God, through Jesus, could now be accessed apart from the temple establishment.

The bottom line is that Christianity, with and without Jesus, attempted to radically subvert the significance and role of the Jewish temple. The irony today is that Christianity, for the most part, has transformed itself into the very commercialized institution that Jesus was trying to bring down. The Vatican, in all its royal pomp and pageantry, has become the temple and the pope, its high priest.

Resurrections and Divinity?

A man named Lazarus walked the earth approximately two thousand years ago. He died and his body was placed in a tomb. After four days, he was resurrected by God and appeared physically, not spiritually, to those who had witnessed his death. Is this resurrection the ultimate evidence of Lazarus's deity?

Before the time of Jesus, the Bible (1 Kings 17) states that Elijah raised a boy from the dead. Second Kings 2 then mentions that Elijah went up to heaven in a whirlwind. Is this evidence that Elijah is God and ultimate proof of the resurrected boy's divinity? If not, then we know at least that heaven has always been open and admissible for born sinners like Elijah. He obviously did not need Jesus's redemptive work on the cross to make it into heaven.

The concept of "resurrection and ascension" is not unique; it occurs frequently throughout the Bible and can even be traced back to early Egyptian mythology. Long before Christians and Muslims, the Egyptians believed in an eternal soul, a resurrection, a last judgment, an afterlife, and a divine mother. The ancient Egyptians, like most contemporary Christians, were obsessed with immortality. The oldest surviving Scriptures in the world—more than 4,300 years old—tell the story of a king who came down from heaven, became a teacher of humankind, died at the hands of conspirators, and appeared again after resurrection.

Osiris, the dead and resurrected god-man, is the most famous deity in the Egyptian pantheon. He became the god of the dead and judge of the souls seeking admission to the afterlife. Eternal happiness greeted those who passed the test; torture and extinction awaited all who failed. Pharaoh was believed to be the Son of Osiris or the Son of Ra or the Son of God. After his death, Pharaoh, a god in human form, rejoined the gods and spent immortality in the heavens. This story should also seem familiar.

The theme of a dead and resurrected god-man recurs throughout ancient mythology. Mythologist Joseph Campbell pointed out that in many cultures there are legends of virgins giving birth to heroes who die and are resurrected (*Joseph Campbell and the Power of Myth*. Six-part mini-series. PBS, 1988).

This could easily lead one to conclude that the biblical account of the resurrection is not the ultimate evidence of Jesus's divinity.

The resurrection story also varies from gospel to gospel and contains numerous contradictions. The gospel of Mark contains no postresurrection appearances at all; it ends with the empty tomb. The resurrection and the belief that Jesus's disciples saw him again after the crucifixion is the greatest miracle known to man. You would think that Mark would have written about it first, or at least mentioned it, but he didn't.

If Jonah's story of surviving three days inside a great fish is clearly a mythical tale, did Jesus really rise from the tomb on the third day? Is the story of Jesus's resurrection merely an adaptation of the god Osiris's resurrection myth? Or, did it derive from the classical Hellenistic idea of the savior as the dead and resurrected son of the great goddess by a virgin birth? There were many such saviors reborn.

Some scholars have suggested that the followers of John the Baptist may have believed that John had risen from the dead shortly after his execution. John's disciples probably thought that John was the Messiah and may have even prayed to him. John's birth, prophetic (messianic) mission, death, and resurrection may have been the model that Jesus's followers used to tell their story.

Was the resurrection story simply created by members of a humiliated and persecuted movement who were desperate for some semblance of vindication? If Jesus really wanted to make a resurrection statement, he should have appeared to the high priest Caiaphas or the Roman prefect Pontius Pilate.

Many biblical scholars have concluded that Jesus's resurrection did not involve his physical appearance among his disciples. They believe that the authors of the Gospels simply used the book of Daniel as a major source in constructing their passion and resurrection narratives. Neither history nor religion nor biblical criticism, however, can prove or disprove the resurrection. People will have to decide for themselves whether it is based on fact, fiction, or faith.

It is interesting to note that the Apostle Paul seems to demand only belief in the resurrection for salvation, whereas the Apostle John seems to demand only belief in the incarnation. Paul refers to Jesus as the Son of God—some scholars argue that he did not believe that Jesus was God incarnate. For Paul, God is the ultimate divine reality of the Old Testament—the eternal God of Israel and creator of the universe—and Jesus was simply his Son (Rom 1:4). According to the gospel of Thomas, salvation is based solely on the understanding of Jesus's secret teachings. What did Jesus say one had to do to inherit eternal life?

Miracles and Divinity?

If laughter is the best medicine, Jesus of Nazareth doesn't stand a chance against contemporary faith healers. I have seen these guys use the power of the Holy Spirit to knock over groups of people like bowling pins! The fact that thousands of Christians in the twenty-first century continue to throw them millions of dollars is ultimate evidence that they are truly great miracle workers. It's the same old con: if someone is supposedly healed, it validates the power of the miracle worker; if a person isn't healed, he or she obviously didn't have enough faith. Of course, contemporary faith healers always have the last laugh; they laugh all the way to the bank!

Are miracles evidence of Jesus's divinity? What supposedly set Jesus apart from other miracle workers was that his power was perceived to emanate from God. Though many religions claim miracles, they probably should not be used to establish the truth of a faith. Hellenistic literature is full of miraculous births, miracle workers, and the resurrection of the dead. Five centuries before Jesus, the Buddha walked on water, ascended to heaven, and then returned to earth.

In the Bible, Elisha restores the dead to life; Jesus raises the dead three times. Elisha feeds a hundred people; Jesus feeds thousands. Elisha heals the water; Jesus walks on water and turns water into wine. Elisha heals leprosy; Jesus heals leprosy. Elisha strikes people (Arameans) with blindness; Jesus strikes Saul (Paul) with blindness. God sends fire from heaven in support of Elijah; God sends a voice from heaven proclaiming Jesus as his Son. Elijah goes up to heaven in a whirlwind; Jesus ascends to heaven on a cloud. There seems to be a noticeable pattern here.

Homer's Odyssey (eighth century BCE) tells the story of how the god Poseidon walked on water and controlled the wind and the waves. The Greeks prayed to Poseidon and called him "the savior." Dionysus, the god of wine, was believed to have made wine from water. The Oracle at Delphi was known for speaking in tongues. During his funeral, a cloud appeared and took Herakles up to heaven amid a glorious display of thunder and lightning. Herakles entered Olympus, the realm of his father Zeus, where he was granted immortality.

Does the fact that Elisha, Elijah, and Jesus performed similar miracles dilute the uniqueness of Jesus and negate miracles as being evidence of his divinity? As one moves from the earliest gospel of Mark to the latter gospels, one can't help but notice that some of the miracles become more exaggerated. Scholars point out that this is the natural progression of legend. Were the stories of Jesus's miraculous powers simply created to distinguish him from all the other prophets, Messiahs, and miracle workers of his day?

The personal name of the biblical God is Yahweh. The name Elijah means "my God is Yahweh." The name Jesus, for many, seems to mean "my God is Jesus." God's name (Yahweh) was later transformed into the title "the Lord." If Jesus is Lord, what is Yahweh's title now?

The Kingdom of God or Heaven?

Did Jesus select twelve disciples (twelve tribes of Israel) to create a new Israel or one apostle (Peter) to establish a new church? According to the Bible, will God save the nation of Israel (the Jews) or the individual Christian Gentile? Will God live with his chosen people in Jerusalem or with Christians in heaven?

It has always been a part of the human psyche to imagine a world without sin and suffering and to invent romances about utopias such as heaven, the kingdom of God, and Shangri-La. Many of us are compelled by faith and the need for psychological security, to believe many things that we cannot prove. The ancient Egyptians believed that heaven was located in the circumpolar stars. The kingdom of God—a Jewish utopia where God would live and rule amongst his chosen people—is an ancient expectation that goes back to the prophets of old. The key to bringing about the kingdom of heaven on earth was to love God and neighbor (Lev 19:18).

Jesus's primary message that the kingdom of God— the will of God on earth as it is in heaven—would soon arrive during the lifetime of some of his followers seems to have been a mistake. God represents absolute perfection and does not make mistakes. Jesus's disciples were expecting the arrival of God's kingdom in Jerusalem; instead, they got the crucifixion.

The Messiah was supposed to restore the world to holiness and redeem the nation. The Jews and Jewish Christians waited, hoped, and longed for the end of suffering. At the end of the day, none of Jesus's disciples or followers lived to enjoy the promised utopia; instead, they experienced execution, persecution, and dispersion.

The kingdom of God never arrived. To save face, was the kingdom of God later reinterpreted as a kingdom of grace, truth, and love—a spiritual kingdom? The second coming of the resurrected Christ was also an event that Jesus's followers expected in their own lifetime. They anxiously awaited his imminent return and the cataclysmic end to the age; but, like the kingdom of God, it never happened.

In historical terms, many believe that Jesus's life was a complete failure. He didn't redeem Israel; he didn't overthrow Rome; he longed for a kingdom that didn't come; he was abandoned by God on the cross; and his teachings, life, and death were distorted by the church. Christians want to believe that Jesus is infallible. Catholics also want to believe that the pope is infallible.

The truth is that our beliefs, especially those that bring us the most comfort, often have nothing to do with reality. The sun appears to rise and set and yet we know that it is a fixed star. Things are rarely what they seem. How can we be so certain about an ineffable God?

The New Testament also informs us that unless you are a Jew, Jesus didn't come for you. And though he was impressed with the faith of some of the Gentiles he encountered and told parables about a good Samaritan, there is no evidence that Jesus ministered to non-Jews.

Jesus specifically stated, "I was sent to the lost sheep of the house of Israel, and to them alone" (Matt 15:24). The twelve disciples represented the twelve tribes of Israel. Jesus's sole mission, according to some scholars, was to liberate and save the Jewish people alone.

If this is true, it would have to be the ultimate religious catastrophe. Jesus comes exclusively for the Jews and they continue to reject him. Some scholars have pointed out that Jesus perceived Gentiles as pigs and dogs (Matt 7:6); they, of course, are the only ones who love and worship him.

Is there really a cause for concern? With the possible exception of a few valid revelations, many scholars believe that most of the information contained in the Bible about God and Jesus are either illusions or distortions. Some scholars also agree that the Christ most people associate with the Gospels is, for the most part, a myth.

Do mythical stories and dogmas impart information or do they simply indoctrinate? It has been said that reading the Scriptures is not a process of discovering facts about God. Can intellect alone find what ultimately can't be found? The true nature of God, his essence, is not merely unknown—it is unknowable (Job 11:7–8).

Is the Holy Trinity Truly Holy?

Does the concept of the Holy Trinity sound like greek to you? Throughout the Gospels, Jesus describes himself as being other than the Father and less than him. In the Old Testament, God clearly identifies himself by making the following statements: "I am the Lord, and there is no other; apart from me there is no God"; "And there is no God apart from me, a righteous God and Savior; there is none but me"; and "I the Lord do not change." How did we get from this clear and concise biblical description of one God to the church's nonbiblical mystery of the Trinity? The Bible clearly warns that no human being can know God in essence or as he is in himself (Job 11:7–8).

Why did it take the church approximately three hundred years to develop and vote on the doctrine of the Holy Trinity? Is this the same institution that insisted the earth was the center of the universe? Interestingly enough, there is no mention of the Trinity in the earliest New Testament manuscripts. And though Jesus taught extensively about God and God's kingdom, nowhere in the New Testament will you find him teaching or discussing the three-in-one concept of the Holy Trinity. How can God, whose hallmark is oneness, be three and one simultaneously?

Did God create humans in his own image or did humans create God in their own ignorance? The ancient Greeks created the gods in their own image but made them immortal. These gods were not perfect but, rather, projections of humankind into a world of fantasy in which everything was possible.

Long before Christianity, Hinduism had developed a Supreme Trinity consisting of three gods—Brahma, Shiva (Siva), and Vishnu—in a single reality. In Buddhism, the spiritual big three is comprised of the Buddha, Dharma, and Sangha. How can a faith like Christianity or Hinduism truly know the exact composition of an indescribable God? Can an infinite God be reduced to a concept that can be expressed in a human word, symbol, or being? The church created and voted on a doctrine to define a Trinitarian God, but does that mean it really exists?

Whether one believes in a divine trio or in a sacred cow, the bottom line is that the magnitude and mystery of God cannot be defined. Did the speculations of the early church simply become the truths of subsequent generations? The reality is that when it comes to God or ultimate truth, he who knows, doesn't know; and he who knows that he doesn't know, knows.

All faiths present themselves as models of religious perfection; nothing could be further from the truth. No faith can claim a monopoly on God or truth. Ultimate truth transcends them all because the unknowable was not meant to be known. Religion, at best, is a poor attempt at expressing an inexpressible reality. In the end, the human intellect is incapable of comprehending the reality of God. All religious knowledge, therefore, has a degree of falseness to it.

> Now it has become clear to me that in our troubled world, so full of contradictions, it cannot be wisdom to assert the unique truth of one faith over another. The wise person makes justice his guide and learns from all. Perhaps in this way, the door may be open again whose key has been lost. (Akbar the Great)

The spiritual path is not to arrive at religious truth, which is impossible, but to arrive at a more accurate understanding of our ignorance. Religion should not seek to impose its perceived truths on anyone. In our attempts to impose our partial religious knowledge on the whole, we inevitably create conflict and fragmentation. Spiritual people are not devoted to issues or causes; they are devoted to God.

The legacy of all religions, however, is that they are different and mutually exclusive; this is why they continue to be so dangerous. In developing sacred Scripture, did humankind create a monster? Will the exclusive claims that permeate these artificial works continue to kill us forever?

Is religion nothing more than a disease born of fear—the fear of being and the anxiety of nonbeing—and the source of untold human misery, as Lucretius suggested? The past as well as the present has consistently proven that when religion is the dominant force in society it always produces horror. Has religion merely evolved into an effective tool of social control by providing the illusion of an afterlife, reincarnation, or enlightenment?

History reveals that the Catholic Church is prone to error. Remember how Copernicus and Galileo over-turned the church-sanctioned view of the earth as the center of the universe? In 1991, the Vatican finally and officially admitted that Galileo had been right and that the church, as well as the Bible, had been wrong.

The Roman Catholic Church initially condemned the heliocentric theory because it contradicted the word of God in the Bible. The Old Testament tells the story of how the Lord aided the Israelite invasion of Canaan by causing the sun to stand still at Gibeon (Josh 10:13). Because the sun is a fixed star, it doesn't make sense that God had to make it stand still.

It is futile to defend the inerrancy of the Bible. If the church's doctrine of the Trinity is also in error, Christianity is in danger of being in violation of God's first and second commandments. Even if the Trinitarian concept is true, the focus of Christianity today is on Jesus, with virtually no emphasis on God the Father—a jealous and avenging God, according to the Bible.

Original Sin and Salvation?

The traditional Christian belief is that Jesus is truly God and truly man. Christianity built its identity on this concept. Christianity also claims to be a religion founded directly by God and to be the only true path to God.

The sad truth, however, is that Jesus was executed for sedition. The early church struggled to make sense of Jesus's shameful crucifixion. Were atonement theories (fall-redemption theology) the result of this struggle to make sense of Jesus's death?

The Torah made normative Israel's experience of alienation (exile), reconciliation (return from exile), death (the destruction of the temple), and resurrection (the reconstruction of the temple). Did Christianity adopt the Torah's theme of exile (separation from God because of original sin), atonement (Jesus's sacrificial death), reconciliation (Jesus's mission of redemption), and renewed covenant with God (the New Testament) to explain the significance of Jesus's life and death?

Fall-redemption theology states that Adam and Eve sinned against God and were subsequently evicted from paradise. God locked the gates and the entire human race lost access to heaven and eternal life. Humankind was lost in sin—eternally separated in spiritual condemnation—and in need of a Savior.

Jesus was God's tremendous plan for salvation. Jesus is a god who came down from heaven for our deliverance. His crucifixion—a perfect sacrifice—effected the remission of sins and redeemed the human race. Jesus, in essence, opened the gates and restored human access to eternal life with God in heaven.

By faith, we can grasp Jesus's victory over sin and be saved; in doing so, we become the elect of God. Jesus's payment for our sin fulfilled his destiny as the Savior of the world. In sum, fall-redemption theology catapulted Jesus from crucified criminal to divine ruler.

Is Jesus really the divine Savior of the entire human race on whom our access to eternal life with God depends? The belief that humankind lost access to heaven because of original sin lacks credibility. A righteous and just God does not punish the innocent for the sins of the guilty.

The atonement of Jesus took place on a wooden cross. The idea that a blood-seeking deity demanded a gruesome human sacrifice in order for humanity to be saved has been condemned as not only irrational but also immoral. The conviction that Jesus's blood cleanses our sins stems from a primitive and barbaric concept of animal sacrifice.

To honor and worship their gods, ancient humans sacrificed living beings so that, from death, life could be reborn. In Mesoamerica, consuming the flesh of sacrificial victims was like consuming the flesh of the gods. This cannibalistic practice seems to parallel the Christian rite of Holy Communion—the eating of Jesus's body and the drinking of his blood. To appease the rain god, Aztec priests killed shrieking children whose tears might induce rain. In the Jewish tradition, sacrifice was the way of dealing with sin.

The idea that we get life from death, rain from tears, sins cleansed by blood, and redemption from human sacrifice is not only primitive and barbaric—it's insane. If a god sacrificed his son in our society today, he would not be sitting on a heavenly throne. He would be sitting either on Death Row or in a mental institution for the criminally insane.

If an immutable and omniscient Jesus understood his mission to be a sacrificial death for the sins of humanity, why did he ask God to take the cup from him at Gethsemane? Why did Jesus believe that God had forsaken him on the cross? Why did he spend an inordinate amount of time and energy preaching a baptism of repentance for the forgiveness of sins, if he was simply going to take away the sins of the world? If Jesus had truly predicted his upcoming execution, why were his followers so shocked by his death?

How can we seriously believe that God is accessible only through Jesus, when the Bible clearly states that Elijah (a supposed born-sinner separated from God) went up to heaven long before Jesus's arrival? Sin existed for tens of thousands of years before Jesus was born. If Jesus's sacrificial death indeed took away the sins of the world, why is pornography a ten-billion-dollar-a-year industry in the U.S. (a predominantly Christian nation) alone? The fact that humans managed to exterminate one hundred million of their opponents in the world wars of the twentieth century was not only a sin against God but against humanity.

If Jesus is the only way, what happened to all those people who did not have access to Mosaic law and died before he came? What is the destiny of a just and righteous Neanderthal who laid down his life for his fellow humans? It's not surprising that many early Christian sects rejected the belief that Jesus's death was a sin sacrifice. They could not fathom the injustice of God inflicting the pain of crucifixion on his innocent Son. On the other hand, there was nothing special about crucifixion in the first century; the Romans literally hammered tens of thousands. Many victims were innocent. Crucifixion wasn't a voluntary program in Judea like it is today in the Philippines.

Was it really necessary for Jesus to be sacrificed in order to make access to eternal life with God possible? In Ezekiel 18:21, God specifically states, "If a wicked man turns from all the sins he has committed and keeps all my decrees and does what is just and right, he will surely live; he will not die." The bedrock of Jesus's teaching and message was repentance, which is in accord with what God had stipulated in Ezekiel 18:21.

There is no doubt that Jesus viewed proper moral behavior (adhering to the commandments) as the key to inheriting eternal life. Jesus said, "Those who have done good will rise to live, and those who have done evil will rise to be condemned" (John 5:29) and "Heaven and earth will pass away, but my words will never pass away" (Luke 21:33).

The self-proclaimed Apostle Paul, who never met Jesus in life, comes on the scene a few years after the crucifixion and literally snatches the "keys to heaven" away from Saint Peter. Many scholars believe that Paul distorted Jesus's primary mission and message. The doctrine of original sin originates with Paul, not Jesus. The impression is that Paul overlaid Jesus's teachings with his "theology of the cross."

For those present at Jesus's execution, the perception was one of a crucified criminal's defeat and death. For those, such as the Apostle Paul, who were not present, the event came to be understood as the victory and salvation of a sacrificial victim. Was Paul responsible for transforming the Jewish Messiah, whom he believed was Jesus, into the dead and resurrected god-man of pagan myth?

Paul believed that God responded to the violence and corruption that enslaved humanity by sending his Son to earth. Jesus broke the enslaving power of sin through his self-giving love and redemptive death on the cross. For Paul, Jesus's crucifixion and atoning death (human sacrifice) was the very embodiment of God's wisdom and power: "The power of God unto salvation" (Rom 1:16). Did Paul simply adopt and modify the theme of a loving father sacrificing his son, from the Old Testament story of Abraham and Isaac?

Paul preached a doctrine of salvation through faith in Christ—the Son of God. It is a salvation based on grace, not works—works cannot save us. Paul believed that no human being could break the power of sin and stand righteous before God. As far as he was concerned, there was absolutely nothing that people could contribute to their salvation.

This belief, however, is in stark contrast with Jesus's primary message of repentance and with what God had stipulated in Ezekiel 18:21 concerning individual responsibility. There is rejoicing in the presence of the angels of God over one sinner who repents. The reality is that loving God, neighbor, and enemy is hard work, which is why most people tend to avoid it. The bottom line is that for Jesus, salvation was based on works (Matt 19:16–19) whereas for Paul, salvation was based on faith not works.

Krishna is the human-incarnate of the god Vishnu—a member of the Supreme Trinity. In Hinduism, the promise of salvation was offered to all people who placed their faith in Krishna—the divine in man. Five centuries before Christianity, Buddhists began placing their faith in the saving grace of the Buddha. They came to believe that they could not achieve salvation based on individual effort or works, so they relied entirely on the grace of the Buddha. Buddhists also believed that the Buddha was an ever-existent eternal being who assumed human form (an incarnation) in order to lead people to salvation. Did Paul adopt a similar theme in his development of Christianity?

Certain sects of Buddhism preferred to worship the manifestation of the Buddha called Amitabha, who was said to reign in a western paradise. He vowed to give salvation to all those who repented of their sins and called upon his name. The state of bliss could be achieved by faith rather than just by asceticism and was, therefore, open to more people.

The Apostle Paul, who was not a direct witness to Jesus's teachings, became the most influential expositor of Christian doctrine. Paul changes the criteria for salvation from observance of Mosaic law to belief in the resurrection. We also find Paul shifting his emphasis from proclaiming Jesus as God's Messiah to Jesus as the Son of God. Was Paul compelled to make this change because the Jews rejected his messianic message? Would the concept of a Jewish Messiah have been irrelevant in the various Gentile communities where Christ would have to compete with Caesar—the son of a God? Was Paul really chosen by Jesus to be an apostle to the Gentiles, or was he simply forced out of Israel?

Paul was a devout Jew who persecuted Christians. He killed for Judaism by attempting to destroy the heretical followers of Jesus Christ. Paul tells us that he met the resurrected Christ while en route to Damascus to arrest and persecute Christians. The Sanhedrin in Jerusalem, however, had no jurisdiction in Syria and, under Roman rule, Jews had no authority to execute the death penalty. Was the greatest conversion in religious history nothing more than a fabrication?

Did Jesus evolve from Israel's messianic redeemer to humanity's Savior the same way Yahweh evolved from a territorial deity to a universally powerful God? Paul postulated the idea of Jesus as the second Adam; he anticipated Jesus's imminent Second Coming; and he also gave a memorable speech concerning Jesus's divinity as the unknown God. Jesus, who was equal to God and God incarnate, suffered the horrific pain of crucifixion for the sins of humanity.

Paul's unfamiliarity with Jesus and Jesus's message does not inspire confidence in him as a reliable source. He was wrong about Jesus's imminent return. Is his "theology of the cross" also mistaken?

Paul virtually reconstituted the Jesus tradition, giving it new meaning, new structure, and new texture. He attached cosmic significance to the crucifixion and resurrection and placed little or no emphasis on Jesus's teachings. His risen Christ seems to have little to do with the historical Jesus.

Paul initially persecuted Jesus's followers. By externally attacking the Jesus movement, did he realize, at some point, that the blood of the martyrs was the seed of the church? Did Paul join the church with the sole intent of destroying it from within? False teachers were stalking the faith and misguided beliefs were corrupting it. The faith was in turmoil: there were new takes on the life, death, and resurrection of Jesus. Christianity became a faith lost in a sea of perspectives.

Many of Paul's letters were devoted to refuting Jesus's original disciples with whom he disagreed. Paul's claims of visionary experiences caused friction among Jesus's initial followers. The Gospels, written after Paul's Epistles, are ironically silent about his letters. Most of the distorted doctrines that plague Christianity today seem to stem from the deceptively beautiful and powerful writings of Saint Paul. The tension between the historical Jesus and the Christ of faith can be traced back to him.

Have we unwittingly been sleeping with the enemy? There is an interesting painting on a church wall that looks, at first glance, like Jesus; up close, however, the face is that of a demonic antichrist. You have to really look to see it. The greatest reality, sometimes, is that which you can't see.

There were early Christian communities who didn't think Jesus's death had any saving value at all and who were not looking for his return. Instead, they emphasized Jesus's role as a teacher over and above his death and resurrection. The early Christians were bound by an oath not to sin. They didn't spin in the neurosis of "sin and salvation" or in "born again" superficiality. Recent tests of "born again" Christians before and after their conversion experiences showed little, if any, difference in their moral behavior.

The story of Adam and Eve in the garden of Eden influenced both Jewish and Christian theology; it is clearly a mythical tale. The story of the garden of Eden was derived from an ancient Sumerian text, *The Epic of Gilgamesh,* one thousand years older than the Hebrew Bible. Sumerian seals from as early as 3500 BCE depict a serpent, a fruit tree, and a goddess giving the fruit of life to a visiting male. Sumerian myths became biblical facts. If the church's doctrine of original sin evolved from myth, what does this say about its doctrine of salvation?

Original sin theology, like the incarnation and Trinitarian doctrines, did not emerge or was not finalized until the fourth century. The belief that all human beings are born in a state of separation from God's loving presence is contrary to Jesus's teachings. If we were separated from God because of sin, why did Jesus say, "The kingdom of God is within you" (Luke 17:21)? The dark theology of original sin—with its false sense of separation—has been the cause of so much human anxiety and unnecessary suffering.

Many Christians no longer accept the idea of an original fall. The Adam and Eve story is not taken literally anymore. Christianity relies on original sin theology because it supports its interpretation of Jesus as a Savior. For Jews and Muslims, the original sin of disobedience is not passed on to humankind. They don't require salvation through the sacrifice of Jesus on the cross. Christian faith and understanding of God as a Trinity of persons also grew out of this early interpretation of Jesus's work of salvation. If Jesus was something less than God, then salvation by his death on the cross would not work.

The incarnation, Trinitarian, and fall-redemption doctrines are interlinked. Today, however, these outdated and misguided dogmas reflect a faith no longer built on solid rock but on distortion. Scores of Christians live under the illusion that the faith stands or falls on these human-made concepts; nothing could be further from the truth. The value of a religion depends upon the timeless truths of its teaching and on its capacity to transform life through love.

For salvation, the Apostle Paul demanded belief in the crucifixion and resurrection (faith in a human sacrifice); the Apostle John demanded belief in the incarnation (the mutability of an immutable God); and both God and Jesus demanded repentance (individual responsibility and ethical behavior). Is salvation based on blood and death or on life and love? Are Christians worshiping God or are they simply worshiping suffering? Is Christianity a sadomasochistic faith as many have suggested?

Lamb of God or Golden Calf?

Is God really three persons in one? Can the human intellect truly understand the nature of an ineffable God? Are we to doubt that Jesus is an incarnate god-figure who

45

is true God and true man? Are we certain that Jesus is coequal and coeternal with the Father?

That God is actually a Trinity of persons is a radical shift and a rather dangerous claim. Many biblical scholars regard belief in the Trinity as obsolete and self-contradictory. If Jesus is not God, Christianity is a cult in violation of God's first two commandments.

Some scholars also maintain that only a small percentage of sayings—roughly twenty percent—in the New Testament can actually be attributed to Jesus. The Jesus in the gospel of John is remarkably different from the Jesus in the Synoptic Gospels (Matthew, Mark, and Luke). The Synoptic Gospels are less explicit in portraying the divinity of Jesus. They tell the story of a humble and inclusive Jesus, whereas the gospel of John depicts a Jesus who is self-exalting and exclusive.

Many scholars agree that the Synoptic Gospels more closely reflect the historical Jesus than the Gospel of John does and that none of the sayings of Jesus in John's Gospel are actually his. Many early Christians rejected the gospel of John as heretical. Contemporary Christians, on the other hand, use John's gospel primarily as a powerful conversion and retention tool.

A recurring theme in mythology is the idea of the mythical rebirth—the transformation of a man into a prophetic, all-powerful, guiding deity. The Buddha lived approximately five centuries before Jesus of Nazareth (the Righteous One). In life, the Buddha only wanted to be a wise man among men. After his death, however, his followers transformed him into a supernatural being and he eventually became known as the Blessed One. Buddhists came to believe that the Buddha was a pre-existent and eternal reality who descended to earth in the form of a human being merely to lead people to salvation.

The Buddha is worshiped almost as a God and believers declare that they will seek refuge only in him. The deification of Confucius immediately followed the transformation of the Buddha. The deification of wise men seems to have been a common occurrence two thousand years ago. Does Jesus fall into this category as well? Is Jesus just another God created by man? Why did humans feel the need to promote Egyptian pharaohs, Roman and Japanese emperors, and wise men to divine status?

Have Christians elevated Jesus to the extent that he now eclipses the one true God? Is this simply a case of mistaken identity in which we killed God's messenger only to deify him later in a false theology of glory? Is the belief that "Jesus is God" an illusion? Are Christians worshiping God in truth when we are, in fact, worshiping Jesus?

Is Jesus really the Lamb of God or just another golden calf? Have Christians merely been deceived by the idolatrous convictions and institutional power needs of an authoritarian church? At the end of the day, what good are two billion Christians if they are worshiping Jesus instead of Jesus's God?

Christianity: A Jesus Cult?

Jesus taught that faith should be built on solid rock. Is Christianity built on solid rock or has it indeed evolved into a Jesus cult? Some scholars argue that the dogmas concerning the nature and relationship between God and Jesus were developed over centuries and are not present in the New Testament.

Did the church consciously and ingeniously transform Christianity into a political ideology and a mechanism of symbolic control? Were Christian stories simply adapted to fit ancient prophecies and the needs of the early Christian communities? The book of Acts tells the story of how Jesus's disciples spoke in tongues on the day of Pentecost. Centuries before the birth of Jesus, the Oracle at Delphi in ancient Greece was known to have spoken in tongues. The Greeks also believed that a golden race existed as holy spirits who protected humans.

Many biblical scholars agree that the Gospels are not accurate. They also insist that the Gospels should not be confused with reality nor interpreted in any literal sense. There are just too many contradictions and embarrassing moral concepts for the text to be divinely inspired. The Gospels should be viewed as portraits and not as historical narratives. The evangelists simply reinterpreted various traditions and myths and included them as part of their gospel story of Jesus.

The image of Jesus would also be reshaped as the church wrote its own version of his birth, life, and death. It has been said that a Christian editor revised the Old Testament in an attempt to make Jesus's life a fulfillment of prophecy. Old Testament passages were frequently distorted, misinterpreted, and quoted out of context in order to create these prophecies for Jesus. The Hebrew canon was also rearranged so that the prophetic books would appear at the end of the text. Did the Christian authors simply extract and modify Old Testament passages, insert them into the New Testament, and then claim divine inspiration?

With the passage of time, spiritual teachings are inevitably altered through the transmission of an oral tradition or through literary translations from one language to another. Different versions of the New Testament were known to be in circulation. The problem with the Old Testament is that it is difficult to determine where interpretive storytelling stops and history begins. The reverse seems to be true with the New Testament; it is difficult to determine where history stops and interpretive story-telling begins.

Was Jesus a God who died to take away the sins of the world, or was he simply a teacher who taught the way of salvation? Jesus's high moral teaching is said to be the heart and soul of his saving ministry. Many believe that it is his message of repentance, love, peace, and brother-hood—not his death or resurrection—which sets us free.

Did the church largely ignore Jesus's teachings in favor of contradictory doctrine and dogma? Many people believe that the church distorted Jesus's primary mission and message, and that these distortions continue to divert attention away from the central issues of his ministry.

Handling the Truth

Has institutional religion really been about God and love or about power, control, and greed? Can a Christianity built on quicksand save itself by abandoning the Christ of faith and reaching for the historical Jesus? Should Christianity be more of a personal search for truth rather than an institution of indoctrination?

Jesus said, "Seek God's kingdom and righteousness" (Matt 6:33). Jesus did not devote himself to a religious es-tablishment, nor did he bury himself in sacred Scripture. He was too busy serving others and doing what he per-ceived to be the will of his God.

Jesus's precise identity is a mystery. There was clearly an enormous power present in his life. His reference to God as *Father* was radical and so were his actions and teachings. Why did a Jewish rabbi disregard the purity laws of his tradition to embrace and heal lepers? Why did he wash the feet of his disciples?

If Jesus was simply echoing the apocalyptic warnings of John the Baptist and the teachings of Hillel or the cynics, why did he draw such large crowds? Why did he teach us to love our enemies and pray for our persecutors? What did he mean when he said, "Man does not live by bread alone"(Matt 4:4)?

How could a tortured man forgive his executioners for nailing him to a wooden cross? How could a Jewish peasant with nothing to give, give two billion people so much? After two thousand years, why are millions of people still fascinated and obsessed with him? I personally can think of no greater teaching, no greater act, and no greater love—can you?

People can be inspired and motivated by Jesus's life and ethical teachings; they don't need Christian mythology to confuse and divide them. That which is truly sacred does not divide; it is doctrinal issues that divide us. Jesus commanded us to love God and each other. He didn't want us spending all our time drowning in a sea of doctrinal disputes.

Nietzsche described Christianity as a faith that looks in a horrible way like a continuous suicide of reason. Church dogma saddles Christianity with a dubious philosophy of uncertain worth and questionable foundation. The early Christians did not accept most of these doctrines, and neither should we. Our attitude toward reality should be open-minded, not dogmatic.

Because of the prevailing climate of doubt (crisis of confidence) concerning the truth of Christianity, traditional Christian theology must be scrapped and reconstructed on a foundation of truth—on solid rock. Jesus turned his tradition and the values of his day upside down—we should endeavor to do the same.

The moral teachings of Jesus and the practicing Christian's experience of God should be the basis of Christian faith. Without change, it is only a matter of time before Christianity joins Greek mythology as an obsolete system of belief. Because Christians are convinced that God is the God of all truth, we will not lose heart—change will inevitably come.

Is the God of Israel the God of all truth or did Jesus reveal that another deity existed who had never been mentioned by the Hebrew Scriptures? Christian theology regarding Jesus's divinity seems to resemble a house of cards. Can the same be said of Judaism's God, Yahweh?

Christianity has its roots in Judaism. The Bible is the ultimate spiritual authority for the Christian faith. Christians used the Old Testament text to interpret Jesus's significance and to create the New Testament. The literal truth of Scripture was a matter of life and death for Christianity itself. But is the Hebrew faith truly built on solid rock?

The Holy One of Israel?

The God of Israel is really many gods (Egyptian, Canaanite, Mesopotamian, etc.) rolled into one. Like the Hindu god Brahma, he is the creator of the universe; like Vishnu, he is a sustainer or preserver; and like Shiva (Siva), he is a destroyer and reproducer. Yahweh eventually becomes the one and only God of Israel. And though he can never be known in himself, the God of the Bible did reveal himself to the prophets. He specifically created prophetic voices to make his will known.

The Holy One of Israel—according to biblical tradition and various scholars—is a partial, murderous, and genocidal land thief who suffers from a multiple personality disorder. Yahweh set Israel apart from all other nations to be his very own; he also bound them to 613 laws. Shortly after God commands the Israelites not to kill, he orders them to exterminate the Canaanites.

The Bible depicts the God of Israel as jealous, demanding, impossible to please, dangerously unpredictable, and always inexplicably angry. Yahweh, in essence, is a warrior deity who fights for and against his own people.

The flood story reveals that God destroyed the world and nearly every person and creature in it, because he saw the great wickedness of his earthly creation. He tested Abraham by demanding that he sacrifice his son as a burnt offering. God also saw a great evil in Sodom and Gomorrah and targeted both cities for destruction.

In Exodus, God resorts to killing the Egyptian firstborn and drowning Pharaoh's army in order to free the Hebrew slaves from bondage. He later has a catastrophic plan to destroy the Hebrews themselves for worshiping a golden calf, but Moses convinces him not to carry it out. And, because of a single display of doubt, Moses was prevented by God from leading the Israelites into the promised land; he dies just in sight of it.

In the conquest of Canaan, God authors a holy war of extermination and adds genocide (ethnic cleansing) to the commandments of the Torah. The Israelites are ordered to slaughter the native Canaanites, to destroy their sacred symbols, and to take their land. The God of Israel has men, women, children, and infants put to death. He is literally a ruthless "baby killer," according to biblical tradition.

God subdues Israel's enemies and rescues his people from hostile foreign powers. He also threatens the Israelites by repeatedly warning them to return to the law and to live in accordance with his will. His punishment for disobedience and stubborn pride comes in the form of terror, destruction, disease, and domination by foreign enemies. There are instances when God actually abandons Israel and hands them over to their enemies (only to deliver them time and again).

The book of Revelation, for many, describes the future of God's wrath and wars. It states that there will be violence and punishment for those who commit great deeds of evil. God plans to ravage humanity and billions will perish as a result. The battle for Jerusalem will eventually take place and then there will be a violent end to the world.

It would take the Israelites centuries to transform their God into a symbol of transcendence and compassion. The God of Israel's unstable personality and future capacity for violence and destruction calls into question the belief that he is a God of love and compassion.

It is impossible to reconcile the God of Noah, who promised that he would never again make war on humanity or destroy the world, with the apocalyptic visions of the biblical prophets. It is interesting to note that Jews, Christians, and Muslims all worship this same God—the God of Abraham.

The Myth of Noah and the Flood?

Thessaly is home to the myth of Deucalion and Pyrrha: an ancient Greek version of the flood story. Zeus, disappointed by the behavior of mortals, decided that humankind needed to be punished. He unleashed a great flood to drown the whole earth. Deucalion, however, was warned about the coming deluge and quickly built an ark. He took his wife Pyrrha and they sat in the ark and waited. Soon it started to rain; it rained until the earth was entirely covered by water.

Deucalion's ark floated over the waters for nine days and nine nights, and eventually came to rest on the top of Mount Onasis. Deucalion and Pyrrha disembarked and immediately offered a sacrifice to Zeus for having saved them. Zeus was so delighted with their offering that he helped them repopulate the earth.

A majority of Americans believe in the story of Noah's ark, the global flood, and God's covenant never to destroy the earth. The great flood associated with the story of Noah's ark is believed to have occurred five thousand years ago. When the floodwaters receded, Noah was approximately six hundred years old. It is believed that he and his sons were responsible for repopulating the entire earth.

Are the biblical flood stories, like the creation accounts, simply myths? Archeologists have found no evidence of a great flood that supposedly occurred in ancient times. Similar flood tales, however, can be found in Egyptian, Mesopotamian, Persian, and Indian mythology. The flood story in the Bible is almost identical to the ancient Babylonian *Epic of Gilgamesh* (tablet eleven). *The Epic of Gilgamesh* is one of the oldest works of literature in the world; it predates the Bible by at least a thousand years.

Gilgamesh was a historical king of Uruk in Babylonia (modern-day Iraq) in and around 2700 BCE. Moses is believed to have written the Pentateuch between 1446 and 1406 BCE. Many of the stories and myths about Gilgamesh, however, were written down from an oral tradition around 2000 BCE. The following is a template of *The Epic of Gilgamesh* (tablet eleven):

In the time before the Flood . . .

. . . resolved to destroy the world in a great flood . . .

. . . build a great boat, its length as great as its breadth, to cover the boat, and to bring all living things into the boat.

. . . gets straight to work and finishes the great boat . . .

. . . loads the boat with gold, silver, and all the living things of the earth, and launches the boat.

. . . orders him into the boat and commands him to close the door behind him. The black clouds arrive . . . all the light turns to darkness. The Flood is so great . . .

The Flood lasts for seven days and seven nights, and finally light returns to the earth.

. . . opens a window and the entire earth has been turned into a flat ocean. . . . boat comes to rest on the top of Mount . . .

. . . the boat lodges firmly on the mountain peak just below the surface of the ocean and remains there for seven days.

On the seventh day: I released a dove from the boat, it flew off, but circled around and returned, for it could find no perch. I then released a swallow from the boat, it flew off, but circled around and returned, for it could find no perch. I then released a raven from the boat, it flew off, and the waters receded . . . it does not circle around and return. I then sent out all the living things in every direction . . .

Many people believe that the story of Noah's flood was divinely inspired. But older, almost identical, Mesopotamian flood stories prove that Noah's ark is really just a biblical spin of the same tale. There are numerous stories, like Noah's ark and the flood, in the Hebrew Bible that parallel older Egyptian and Mesopotamian tales.

The story of Noah's flood has passed over into mythology. Knowing this, can we honestly maintain a commitment to the authority and infallibility of the Bible as God's word in written form? Is the Bible the result of divine inspiration or human plagiarism or both?

The Myth of Abraham and a Chosen People?

Abraham is the founding figure of Judaism, Christianity, and Islam. The Hebrews believed that God had chosen them as a special people because Abraham responded to God's calling. Judaism traces its roots to a covenant, or binding agreement, between God and Abraham: Israel would be God's kingdom and Abraham's descendents would become his servant people and treasured possession in the promised land.

It is believed that Abraham lived approximately four thousand years ago. It is also believed that Abraham was the first to proclaim that there was only one God who ruled the universe. This God, who created the heavens and the earth, gave Abraham a special mission. God commanded Abraham to go to a new land and promised him that future generations of his descendants would inherit that land.

According to the Torah, the Hebrews lived near Ur in Mesopotamia. In 2000 BCE, they migrated, herding their flocks of sheep and goats into a region known as Canaan (modern-day Israel). Canaan was the promised land given to Abraham and his descendents by God to be theirs alone. It is there that God ordered Abraham to kill his son in a blood sacrifice and to burn his body as an offering.

Is Abraham, like Noah, a mythical figure? Modern archaeology has found nothing from the middle Bronze Age (2000–1500 BCE) directly associated with Abraham or his offspring. All respectable archaeologists have given up hope of proving Abraham's existence.

A few religious leaders, like Zoroaster in Persia and the Egyptian ruler Akhenaten, believed in a single powerful deity. In 600 BCE, the Persian prophet Zoroaster founded a new religion based on monotheism. Zoroaster rejected Persia's old gods in favor of a single wise god who ruled the world.

In a flash of inspiration in 1380 BCE, the Pharaoh Akhenaten began to have monotheistic tendencies, which was a massive break with Egyptian tradition. The Pharaoh attacked polytheism by desecrating the inscriptions and images of the old gods of Egypt. He tried to sweep away all other deities by introducing and promoting the worship of Aten—the one true God. This was the world's first recorded expression of monotheism.

Akhenaten's radical introduction of a new religion based on the worship of a single deity, however, was short-lived. Immediately after his death, Egypt reverted to polytheism. What happened to Akhenaten's monotheistic cult? Were they converted, executed, enslaved, or exiled? Did they go to Canaan and become the Israelites? It is interesting to note that Akhenaten's name was encoded in a Dead Sea Scroll. Did Israel (ISis-RA-EL) derive its name from Isis (Egyptian goddess), Ra (Egyptian god), and El (Canaanite god)?

The culture and religion of ancient Egypt was so powerful and influential that over time their neighbors copied much of it. Did the stories of Abraham and

Muhammad attacking their polytheistic traditions in favor of monotheism originate from the historical events surrounding Egypt's Pharaoh, Akhenaten?

Ancient Egyptian literature includes hymns, prayers to the gods, proverbs, love poems, and depictions of royal victories in battle. In one of the tombs, there is a hymn composed by Akhenaten himself; sections of the hymn are strikingly similar to certain verses in the Bible's Psalm 104. There are many parallels between Akhenaten's ideas and those found in the Bible. Many scholars believe that it was the ancient Egyptians who taught monotheism to the Jewish people. Some scholars also believe that the Jewish people have their origins in Egypt and not Mesopotamia.

The Myth of Moses and the Ten Commandments?

A majority of Americans believe that Moses really did part the Red Sea so that the Israelites could escape their Egyptian captors. Moses is revered as the first and greatest of the prophets. The exodus from Egypt and the conquest of Canaan is believed to have occurred between 1499 and 1400 BCE. According to Jewish tradition, Moses was a great spiritual leader who received the law from God on Mount Sinai. The Ten Commandments have guided Israel throughout its history.

The Hebrews believed that God made a covenant with Moses. Under the agreement, the Jewish people accepted God as the sole ruler of heaven and earth and, in return, the Lord made them his chosen people. Judaism is a religion derived from God's revelation to Moses at Mount Sinai. The Ten Commandments outlined religious duties toward God and rules for moral conduct toward other people. Religious Jews keep the law as God-given and perceive it as the embodiment of the divine will.

Egyptian, Sumerian, Babylonian, Persian, and Greek traditions greatly influenced the mythology and religion of the ancient Israelites. Moses' story begins with his mother abandoning him in a basket along the banks of the river Nile. It is interesting to note that other great leaders in the ancient Middle East, such as Sargon of Akkad (2300 BCE) and Cyrus II of Persia (died 529 BCE), were saved in infancy by being set afloat in a basket. As a matter of fact, more than thirty variations of these "baby in a basket" folktales survive today.

A Babylonian king by the name of Hammurabi lived between 1790 and 1750 BCE. He is best known for his code of laws. The Code of Hammurabi is not only a remarkable set of laws—it is the first major collection of laws in history. The code deals with murder and theft and follows the principle of "an eye for an eye" and "a life for a life." Did the concept of the Ten Commandments derive from Hammurabi's code of laws?

Some scholars have suggested that Moses's Ten Commandments story was plagiarized from Zoroaster's *Persian Book of Law* or from *The Egyptian Book of the Dead* (The Negative Confessions). They also insist that Moses's story cannot be taken literally because it is a complete copy of other myths with the names and places changed. If Jesus's story in the New Testament and Muhammad's story in the Qur'an were patterned after Moses, what does this mean?

Many scholars believe that ancient Israel, as described in the Hebrew Bible, never existed. They contend that there is no archeological evidence to corroborate the biblical account of Hebrew slaves in Egypt, their release by a Pharaoh after a series of plagues, an Egyptian military catastrophe, or the existence of Moses. The actual location of the biblical Mount Sinai has also never been found.

Many scholars also agree that the biblical saga of Israel is not a miraculous revelation but a brilliant product of the human imagination compiled and shaped by Hebrew scribes after their Babylonian exile. It is believed that the Hebrew Bible was composed in the middle of the first millennium BCE—more than a thousand years after many of the events it purports to narrate. Adam, Eve, Noah, Abraham, and Moses are said to be merely fictional characters in Hebrew mythology.

The Word of God?

The Holy Bible is the most revered book in human history and remains the foundation of faith for two–thirds of the world's population. It is believed that the text contains the sacrosanct words inspired by the divine. A majority of Americans believes the Bible is literally true and not just a book of stories meant to be interpreted as symbolic lessons.

The Hebrew Bible is a record of Jewish religious experience. The traditional belief is that Moses wrote the Torah between 1446 and 1406 BCE. For millions of people, the Bible is the word of God. As God's revelation, it is the means of communicating a number of divinely related truths, which could not otherwise be known.

The reality is that you can't establish the authority of a book any better than by saying God wrote it. The Bible is not only a record of ancestral contact with the divine—it is an epic saga of conflict, deliverance, and redemption. It has become a tool for understanding history and human nature. For devout Jews, keeping the Torah is the pathway to God.

Many biblical scholars, on the other hand, believe that Judaism derived theological value from converting myth into history. The Hebrew Bible is said to be a collection of myths—a fusion of ideas, stories, traditions, and chronologies that were written and rewritten over a span of a thousand years or more. The text is true in some ways and not in others; the stories are not true in every detail.

Some scholars claim that ancient scribes invented biblical history and that the Bible evolved from a collection of polytheistic myths and legends from various cultures into a mostly coherent monotheistic account of Israelite history. Because many of the biblical stories cross the boundary separating legend from history, one has trouble deciding where interpretive storytelling stops and history begins. It is also impossible to determine what proportion of the revealed text contains the sacred word of God and how much of it is the work of mortal minds. Has humankind been interpreting and reinterpreting myth instead of truth all this time?

Many contemporary scholars also reject the view that Moses actually wrote the Torah. The different writing styles contained in the text reveal that many authors wrote it. Contradictory passages in the Torah also make it highly unlikely that Moses was the sole author. Some stories are told twice with conflicting details: there are two creation accounts and two flood stories. Scholars have suggested that the creation account was simply borrowed from an ancient Sumerian tale (*The Epic of Gilgamesh*).

It is believed that the sacred texts began to be written in Hebrew from an oral tradition in the ninth century BCE. Some stories, however, can be traced back to the eleventh century BCE. In 622 BCE, the book of Deuteronomy was mysteriously found deep within the temple; from that point on, Yahweh could only be worshiped at the temple in Jerusalem. The formation of the Pentateuch is believed to have occurred between 586 and 450 BCE. The oldest known biblical text, however, dates to the third century BCE.

After the Babylonian destruction of the temple in 587 BCE, the Jewish people had to rethink their past and retell their story. It is likely that Hebrew scribes, exiled in Babylon, wrote the story of Exodus. The myth of Exodus engendered hope for the future. The folk tales concocted by the priests were designed to lift their spirits while in captivity; later, they were passed down into history. The scribes attempting to organize their tradition found it impossible to write a historically accurate account of what happened more than seven hundred years before their time.

The Jews were a chosen people on the verge of extinction in Babylon. Scribes wrote down stories about their ancestors and tried to make sense of their own world. What did the Israelites do to lose God's favor? What happened at Mount Sinai was key to why they were in trouble with God. For them, the most important truth of all was how God gave Moses the law, which people were to observe for all time.

Prophets also emerged to interpret God's will. During their exile in Babylon, the people of Israel saw the words of their prophets fulfilled. They had lost favor and were in trouble because they had violated the covenant and sacred laws of their God.

After the Babylonian captivity, editing and inserting stories into the Pentateuch became an integral part of Jewish tradition. The idea of divine inspiration of Scripture, however, seems to have emerged rather slowly and piecemeal. In the second century BCE, the idea that the writers of the Bible were divinely inspired and that everything in the sacred text was true began to emerge. Divine inspiration gradually spread to the whole of the Bible. The Jews now had a powerful new weapon: a book authored by God himself.

And though each of the Jewish prophets had experienced God differently, they all performed a similar function: they interpreted God's will, confronted political and religious establishments, and predicted the future. The prophets were not speaking their own words, but the word of God. The problem, however, was that the various prophetic messages, supposedly from the same divine source, contradicted one another rather frequently.

Isaiah and other prophets predicted the great restoration of Israel after its return from exile, but it never happened. The prophet Haggai also said that the Jew who helped lead Israel home from exile in Babylon would be used by God to destroy other nations. Instead of victory over other nations, however, Israel was conquered and oppressed by one foreign empire after another.

The promises God made through Isaiah, Haggai, and earlier prophets had clearly not been kept. The failure of prophecy, and the emphasis that continues to be placed on it, is extremely disturbing. In those instances where prophecies seemed to have been fulfilled, we find that they were simply manufactured after the event had occurred and projected back in time.

The concept of salvation also surfaces in the second century BCE. The dead will be resurrected and judged: the good will go to heaven and the evil will go to hell. Holiness is in the here and now, but salvation comes at the end of time. What shifted was the redefinition of salvation from the here and now to the end time. For those who accepted their guilt and changed their ways, there was hope. By the time of Jesus, the message of salvation had largely evolved from God saving his people Israel to that of an individual pursuit.

In 600 BCE, Zoroaster taught that, in the end, God would triumph over the forces of evil. On that day, all individuals would be judged for their actions. Those who had done good would enter paradise and those who had done evil would be condemned to eternal suffering. Zoroastrianism had a significant impact on Judaism, Christianity, and Islam.

During the exile in Babylon, at the time of the second temple and during the rule of the Persian and Hellenistic monarchs, new elements were added to the Hebrew Bible. Scribes continually expanded and clarified the text. The tradition of ascribing human emotions to Yahweh also continued. The reformers rewrote Israelite history down to its final editing in the time of Ezra and Nehemiah.

The editing of these writings required more than nine centuries to reach their final form. Some scholars believe that Ezra, a priest, is the elusive editor and consolidator of the five books of Moses. The mystery of who was responsible for writing the first chapters of the Bible, however, may never be fully resolved.

Many scholars remain skeptical of the historical value of the biblical writings. Modern scholarship continues to dispute many stories of the Exodus. As far as they are concerned, the book of Exodus is merely a folktale created centuries later in another time and place. The events that Exodus spoke of never happened. The desert could not have supported the vast number of Israelites reported in the Bible: an estimated six hundred thousand to three million people. There is simply no archaeological evidence to corroborate the story of an exodus from Egypt or an Israelite conquest of Canaan.

The Bible tells the story of how the Israelites entered Canaan, defeated the people there, and claimed the land that God had promised them. The Lord aided the invasion and fought for his chosen people by drying up the Jordan River, bringing down the walls of Jericho, and causing the sun to stand still at Gibeon. The text says that Joshua conquered Jericho, a fortified oasis, after its stone walls miraculously crumbled. Archaeological evidence, however, suggests that there was no walled city at the time. As a matter of fact, the lack of evidence of sudden destruction at several key sites contradicts the biblical account of Joshua leading the Israelites to military victory.

Because of a lack of evidence, many scholars completely reject the biblical story of a military conquest of Canaan. The current consensus is that Israel arose out of a gradual and relatively peaceful infiltration. According to historical and archaeological evidence, the Israelites never invaded Canaan at all but were, in fact, Canaanites themselves. Israelite and Canaanite language, religion, and culture are strikingly similar.

Historical evidence also suggests that the Israelites initially lived on the fringe of Canaanite society. They were indigenous countercultural Canaanites whose customs evolved in response to social and economic conditions and who eventually came to dominate the region as a people. They became a nation not by fighting battles, but by telling stories. Traditional Hebrew contempt for Canaanites—their longstanding adversaries in the promised land—is reflected only in their writings. The Bible is said to be a cultural fiction: the stories were shaping the people as much as the people were telling the story.

In the Torah, Israel suffered through exile, found atonement, attained reconciliation, and renewed its covenant with God. The Judaic system of the Torah made normative the experience of alienation and reconciliation; exile and return became the structure of all Judaism. The reality, however, is that only a minority of "Israel" had in fact undergone these experiences: some Jews were never in exile (no alienation) and some Jews never returned from exile (no reconciliation).

Is the Bible a real historical book or is it simply a vehicle expressing a religious philosophy and a guide to how the Israelites should live? Revelation within the sacred Scriptures is rare and often overwhelmed by distorted human projections and primitive superstitions. What imagination is to art, revelation is to religion; often, fancies are mistaken for facts.

The biblical text combines historical information with symbolic imagery. Once the Bible begins to be interpreted literally instead of symbolically, the idea of its God becomes impossible. The problem is that the Bible both reveals and distorts God.

Is the idea of God as an author of holy books simply a myth? Many believe that the Bible is not the word of God in any literal or verbal sense, and that the texts are not divinely inspired, inerrant works. For them, the biblical stories are only myths.

Many of the biblical events are almost certainly not historical; we find history systematically selected. The Pentateuch's narrative is not an experience interpreted but invented. It spoke of events that had never happened.

The discovery of the Dead Sea Scrolls revealed that different versions of the Hebrew text were in circulation. The Bible's meaning has always been open to interpretation. Certain sects of Judaism abandoned much of the original Torah because they no longer found it to be relevant. More recent sects of Judaism have moved further and further from the notion of the Torah as their divinely inspired, authoritative text.

The plagiarism and contradictions prevalent throughout the Bible prove its human origin. Did the Jewish priests merely create a religious system to ensure they were well fed, paid, clothed, and married? The high priest and his allies were the most wealthy and influential of all Jewish groups.

Was the Torah simply an artistic triumph in psychological deception and falsification? Did the sacred text oppress and exploit the Jewish people for centuries, or did it play a key role in their survival? The power of the priests shaped the worldview and way of life of the Jewish nation; the Bible was the source of their authoritative control.

The Jews perceived their world in this way for a very long time. It is as if they spent their lives trying to live out a cosmic myth. Many rabbis also colluded in this oppression and took no care of the poor. They would eventually retreat from the urgent social problems of the community into the sacred texts. It is also interesting to note that the general rabbinic expectation concerning the nations of Gentiles is negative—rabbis consigned Gentiles to annihilation.

In the final analysis, Judaism is a human construct comprised of borrowed ideas from various traditions and myths. The Bible appears to be a text where myth masquerades as history, where legend rubs shoulders with fact, and where the best stories prove to be the least reliable. Is the Bible simply a book of war and a book of hate as some have suggested? Hatred of enemies and abundant acts of atrocity can be found on page after page of the Hebrew Scriptures.

Many Jews continue to interpret the Bible literally. In the Torah, God promised the land to the descendants of Abraham and thus gave Jews a legal title to Palestine. For them, Jerusalem is the gateway to heaven. They also believe that God chose them out of all nations to be a light to the world by spreading knowledge of the law. Israel continues to have a heightened sense of its status as an elected people with a supernatural standing in God's plan for creation and the history of humanity.

The reality, however, is that a universal God does not favor one group of people over another, nor does he hand out legal titles to land. God's word is not confined to any location, culture, language, or religion. Love has no chosen people because love knows no separation. The idea of God promising land to one group of people at the expense of another is absurd. World tension stemming from the ongoing Middle East crisis is based on nothing more than a Jewish mythical belief that their God gave them the land of Israel.

The traditional belief of a chosen people and a promised land is an illusion. The Israelites, Aztecs, and numerous other sacrificial cults all regarded themselves as God's chosen people. Many Jews and Christians, however, continue to believe that unless the Jews settle in the whole land of Israel—as defined in the Bible—there can be no redemption. The annexation of land—including territory at this time belonging to Palestinian Arabs—has become the supreme religious goal of many ideological groups. Zionism, like manifest destiny, uses the Bible to grab land and sanctify genocide.

The Palestinians have a legitimate case against Israel—they have lost their country. Jerusalem is a city cursed by religious enmity and the Holy Land continues to be a place where one hates one's fellow man to the greater glory of God.

Islam—the Perfect Faith?

Islam means "submission to God" and is the third major religion to emerge from the Middle East. Islam remains a powerful influence in the world today and is currently the second largest religion on the planet. Over a billion of the earth's people are Muslims. As the world's fastest growing religion, Islam is currently experiencing a global resurgence.

The prophet Muhammad is the founder of Islam. Although Muslims honor Muhammad, they do not worship him as a god. Muslims believe that Muhammad is the last and most important prophet of God.

The Qur'an is the word and will of God delivered to the prophet Muhammad by the angel Gabriel in the seventh century. Millions of Muslims refer to the Qur'an daily to explain their actions and to justify their aspirations. The Qur'an is Islam's miracle; it is a book of divine revelation that is God's representation on earth.

Muslims believe that Islam is the perfect faith, that Muhammad is the perfect prophet, and that the Qur'an is the perfect holy text. Muslims also believe that the Qur'an is the only perfect copy of a heavenly text written by God—a text that Jews and Christians misinterpreted, corrupted, and distorted. The Qur'an is a revelation that corrects the errors of both the Hebrew and Christian scriptures and must be read literally as the absolute and unchanging word of God.

Scholars, on the other hand, believe that the Qur'an is merely a product of salvation history, an ad hoc text created late in an era and projected backwards in time.

Scholars point to the fact that no Qur'anic material exists from the first century of Islam. Many members of Muhammad's inner circle were killed in the battles that led to the expansion of the Islamic Empire. Valuable knowledge of Qur'anic revelations died with these men. The first compilers of the Qur'an collected fragments of information and did their best to consolidate what they could find. Muslims argued over what constituted Qur'anic Scripture and what did not.

Some scholars argue that if the Qur'an is indeed God's perfect and unchanging word, how can the difference between manuscripts of the Qur'an in circulation today be reconciled with those recently discovered in Yemen? The manuscripts of the Qur'an found in Yemen are said to be the oldest known copies in existence. Scholars noticed key differences of extreme significance such as variant readings and verse orders. A similar impact of this magnitude in Christianity would be like someone suddenly finding the skeletal remains of Jesus.

According to some scholars, if the Qur'an is an evolving document, which the discovery in Yemen seems to prove, then fourteen centuries of Islam as a religion and a way of life has essentially been meaningless. For them, the discovery of the Yemeni Qur'ans breaks the only legitimate leg Islam had to stand on because the Qur'an is what called the religion into existence.

Like the Bible, the Qur'an has its share of contradictions and calls to violence in the name of God. It clearly states that Muslims are required to wage holy wars against non-believers (non-Muslims), and that peace is possible only for those (Muslims) who follow the straight path.

The Qur'an draws on the same beliefs and stories that appear in the Bible. In the Qur'an, Isaac becomes Ishmael, Moses becomes Muhammad, Mount Sinai becomes Mount Hira, the Exodus becomes the Hijra, and the Ten Commandments become the Qur'an itself.

Muhammad accepted the original teachings of Jewish and Christian scriptures as God's word. In the Qur'an, Jesus foretells of Muhammad as his successor. Can this be true? Muslims believe that Jesus was a prophet. What is a prophet? A prophet is a person who speaks by divine inspiration, revealing or interpreting the will of God. A prophet is one who foretells future events.

In Luke 13:33, Jesus says, "For surely no prophet can die outside of Jerusalem!" Did the prophet Muhammad die outside of Jerusalem; if so, what does this mean? It is interesting to note that Moses, Muhammad, and Joseph Smith all died outside the "eternal capital" of Israel.

A Final Analysis

The problem in the world today is that everyone views their religion as literal facts and everybody else's as imaginative constructs. The reality, however, is that all religions are artificial constructs of the human imagination. The view that "my faith is right and everyone else's is wrong" continues to be responsible for more misery, destruction, and death than any other force in human history. Our myths, perceived as truths, are killing us.

The present is becoming an enemy of the past—undermining the truths of Judaism, Christianity, and Islam. Judaism was obviously not built on solid rock. The Bible's overwhelming irrationalism is too significant to ignore. Because Christianity and Islam share a common origin with Judaism (the mythical Abraham), they too are on "shaky" ground.

Christianity draws heavily on Judaism, retaining the Hebrew Scriptures as part of its Bible known as the Old

Testament. Because of its stance on biblical literalism and inerrancy, Christianity has painted itself into a corner.

Many Jews spend their lives trying to live out a cosmic myth, whereas many Christians spend their lives trying to be "Christ-like." Do people suffer when they are unable to imitate or conform to a particular pattern of perfection? In conforming to a pattern, or religious tradition, one is never free. One is, instead, educated or indoctrinated to live in a field of division and conflict.

Many scholars believe that the Western worship of God—Judaic, Christian, and Islamic—is simply the worship of a literary character or mythical figure; and, as with all mythical figures, facts aren't as important as beliefs. Inspiration doesn't seem to stem from a direct experience of the divine but from myths passed down from generation to generation.

Is the God of monotheism merely an illusion? If God is not the brutal, partial, and murderous God of Israel or the Christian fabrication of the Holy Trinity, who is *Our Father which art in heaven*?

CHAPTER 2

Truths That Set Me Free

I N THE beginning, a primitive man looked at the sun, moon, and stars and wondered what they were. He didn't know what to make of thunder, lightning, rain, volcanic eruptions, earthquakes, floods, tornados, and the fertility of the earth. We know from early cave paintings that powerful animals were depicted as gods. Religion seems to have evolved from primitive animism to polytheistic and monotheistic mythology.

All-powerful and immortal deities go back at least eleven thousand years; great goddesses seemed to have emerged a thousand years later. Many of these gods received their personalities from the animals they had once been.

When man was nomadic, his gods were free spirits; when he decided to stay put and work the land, he imprisoned his gods in temples. Over time, certain cultures would merge all their gods, and their individual attributes, into one deity. Eventually, they proclaimed themselves to be religions of salvation through which one could live a life after death by following certain rituals and devoting oneself to a savior god.

Early man was also baffled by dreams, hallucinations, illness, and death. They were just as terrified of death as we are today. With the changing of the seasons, trees and plants seemed to live, die, and then live again. The sun died each night as it vanished into darkness and then reemerged in a resurrection of light at the dawn of each new day. When one human died, the remaining wondered where life went. Believing in an afterlife, they buried the dead with their personal items and the things they would need in the next life.

In order to approach the gods properly, powerful priesthoods eventually emerged. In their attempts to appease the gods, priests performed the required sacrifices and chanted the needed prayers. In most early forms of sacrifice, an animal—in some cases, a human—offered its life on a sacred chopping block or altar. A system of cosmological conceptions, magic rites, and divinatory practices gradually developed. Priests also interpreted the divine will and requested favors from the gods. They held much of the fertile land, possessed unheard of wealth, and built numerous temples.

Some men and women may have also experienced revelations from God. It is interesting to note that comparable stories—stories of creations, virgin births, incarnations, resurrections, second comings, and last judgments—can be found in many distinct cultures and traditions. Why do we think about God and why do we tell similar stories? Is it simply human nature or did God leave his imprint on our souls (the God gene)?

Which came first, God or the human need for God? Did humans create gods and goddesses in an attempt to understand and control the world? In our desire for ultimate security, in our longing to satisfy our deepest aspirations, and in our attempt to explain the tragedy and pain of life, did we create the idea of God? Did the concept of a supreme being and the possibility of eternal life enable us to bear the terror of existence and the horror of nonexistence? Or did humans create the idea of God from cues sent from heaven?

Is the history of God nothing more than the evolutionary consciousness of the faithful? Some scientists believe that the need for God may be a crucial trait stamped deeper and deeper into our genome with every passing generation. Perhaps religion is simply a product of evolution. Scientists also believe that the concept of God is preloaded into our genome because it helps us deal with the reality of our death. The God gene, which produces a God experience, is simply a built-in pacifier that enables us to tolerate our inevitable demise.

Personal Truths about God

After years of searching, I have come to realize that no one can prove that God exists, and no one can prove that God does not exist. Absence of evidence is not evidence of absence. I would like to believe that a cosmic mind was responsible for the Big Bang and the evolution of all that exists. Pascal's wager begins to make sense at this point. I choose to believe in God.

Although no definition of God is to be equated with God, I believe that God is an immanent spirit who transcends human understanding. The greatest need in people's lives today is to discover the true identity of God. The reality, however, is that the identity and nature of God cannot be known. God, the source of all being, is all things to all people and different things to different people.

Everyone can seek God. The prophets demand that we care for and love one another and, in doing so, find God. The emphasis is placed on active service as a path to the realization of God.

The hidden God reveals himself to anyone who seeks him. While all of us are divinely inspired to look for God, none of us are remotely capable of fully comprehending the unfathomable God we are seeking. People must work out for themselves exactly what God is. Each person must apprehend the truth for herself. It has been said that a Christian who truly begins to find God realizes that the one who is found is not at all the one who was sought. All efforts to go from the general to the specific will be in vain; you will find yourself going from the specific to the general in an honest search for God.

Seeking God in solitude began to have meaning for me. I study the scriptures with the intensity of a seeker—sifting fact from fiction. Truth can only be unearthed in thoughtful examination and reexamination. For many, however, the pursuit of ultimate truth is like gathering flowers. Bertrand Russell noted that the flowers grow only at the beginning of the road and disappear long before we have reached our journey's end.

The only reliable knowledge of God comes in the form of a spiritual epiphany or revelation. This is a personal religious experience that cannot be adequately explained. We know it and yet it is not known. One cannot know God, but one can have "a knowing" of God. Faith loses its meaning after such an experience. God's revelation of his presence is the only valid starting point for thought about God.

Spiritual Epiphany and Revelation

A spiritual epiphany or revelation is a direct encounter between a divine element and a human element. God, in some sense, speaks in a voiced silence. This mystical encounter with God is utterly indescribable. For thousands of years, men and women have experienced a dimension of the spirit that seems to transcend the world (the God gene?). The theologian, Karl Barth, saw revelation as a dynamic event in which God is personally involved. He said that revelation comes to humans in the same way a tangent line touches a circle.

Heavenly sparks are struck when a holy soul is touched by the infinite and it comes to realize that it has truly found the living God. There is a sudden and un-expected illumination. Words cannot express what hap-pens in the soul when someone is in the presence of the sacred. There is nothing rational about this overpowering experience. All we can do is describe how we felt after the encounter. It is simply an unconscious psychological element of religious experience.

This intense experience of mystery is the only way to verify a reality that lies beyond the human intellect. Our proof of the existence of God must derive from our experience of God. The meeting of God and human is a mystery and must remain so; it is also a certainty that provides its own confirmation through the effects it has on the human. This meeting is a matter of a person choosing and being chosen.

Our encounter with God, through revelation, brings its own proof. Revelation is God's way of telling humans that he exists; it is also a human's way of telling himself and others about the reality of God. God's existence is not a matter of logical or scientific demonstration but of inner awareness. One cannot dismiss the realm of reli-gious experience and belief as illusory. If there is a God, there is a God—whether one acknowledges him or not.

Religion, unfortunately, has a tendency to enslave and distort revelation by reducing it to a code, a creed, or a book. The divine reality experienced in revelation is almost always replaced by a concept of God that has arbitrarily and willfully been formed under the influence of organized religion. The person who has had a mystical experience knows that all the symbolic expressions of it are faulty. Many people believe that an awareness of God's presence is a sure sign of salvation and that it is futile to rely on external authority and scripture. The key, however, may be in analyzing religious experience and extracting from it the essence of religion.

God conveys commands to human beings via something analogous to telepathy or thought transference. There is then a human attempt to anticipate what God in his revelation wills us to do. God never tells us specifically what he is asking of us. We experience him simply as a presence and an imperative, and we have to work out the meaning for ourselves. There are, however, insights that arise from profound thought and experience.

Encountering God is an exhilarating experience, but it makes demands on the individual who meets him. Life from that moment forward is never the same. There is both a sense of this being an enormous moment and a desire to escape from it.

Some scientists, however, claim that our most profound feelings of spirituality may be due to little more than an occasional shot of intoxicating brain chemicals governed by our DNA. The God gene is believed to be directly related to our level of self-transcendence. Such feelings can lead to an intuitive sense of God's presence. This feeling of transcendence may launch a quest for God or simply a belief in God.

Religion and Sacred Scripture

The truth about religion and sacred scripture is that we made most of it up and then pretended like we didn't. Religion does not yield final, unanimous answers. It is wishful thinking to believe that one's faith actually reaches the mind of God or the beginning of the world. Over time, the speculations that we derived from our mystical encounters with God (the God gene?) became sacred truths.

Religion is an attempt to engage the ultimate and express an inexpressible reality. It is revelation and illusion produced by psychological projection. The goal of any religious endeavor is union with the absolute. Because it grasps at God, religion is a contradiction of revelation. Carl Jung believed that religion was a defense against the experience of God. For many, religion is not a mirror of reality but rather a distortion.

Religion also attempts to address matters of ultimate meaning in human existence. It tells stories that it believes will connect us to God. No religion, however, can contain all of God's possibilities and truths. Religion shapes the world of its believers by identifying the questions and providing answers that people know to be true.

Religion takes advantage of the fact that life is both drama and trauma. Everyone has a moment of realization when their poverty, suffering, insecurity, and brokenness is acknowledged. There is also a dark night of the soul and the pain of abandonment. Without God and the possibility of an afterlife, death is horrific. This is why we find so much comfort in the idea of a savior.

When life hurts and dreams fade, nothing helps like hope; and where there is hope, there is religion. The kingdom of God and other messianic and apocalyptic expectations were all born from suffering. These beliefs provided the illusion of hope and an escape from the harsh reality of daily life.

Clergy has often taken advantage of the inevitable reality of sin and guilt. Guilt has been the source of so much of the church's power and control. Guilt can drive a person toward a feeling of condemnation and self-rejection. Indoctrination begins with self-contamination: one is sinful at birth, corrupt in life, and evil in every natural impulse. Hell, not heaven, has dominated the imagination of the church and its followers.

The clergy also benefits from the deep-rooted anxiety that is part of the human condition—a confused soul looking for guidance in a time of crisis. Suffering, which is an inescapable part of life, is said to be a consequence of sin and disobedience. The clergy pretends to offer psychological and spiritual security through a system of rewards and punishments. They have, for the most part, duped people into believing that they alone have access to God and can mediate his forgiveness.

Religion is not only an effective form of social control, it is big business. Doing the will of God is really doing whatever the clergy desires. Religion continues to be attractive, because it promises such things as a kingdom of God, a messiah, an apocalypse, an afterlife, a reincarnation, and an enlightenment.

Religious leaders promise things that they cannot prove exist; they simply guarantee the various illusions they've created. Only by actually dying will one experience an afterlife, reincarnation, enlightenment, or annihilation; it is the only way of knowing or not knowing.

Throughout history, the clergy have lived lavishly, receiving tithes and first fruits, while the ignorant and destitute suffer in their sins. Religious organizations continue to claim far too much for their view of God. They also make extraordinary demands on the world at large. It has been said that religion is nothing more than an attempt by humans to rule fellow humans under a distant, high, and all-powerful God.

Jesus, for Christians, was the perfect answer to the questions concerning the meaning of life and human destiny. He brought comfort and salvation to a desperate world and the wonderful possibility of eternal life with God in heaven to the hopelessly mortal. In light of their own mortality, Christians took comfort in the belief that in the death and resurrection of Jesus, God had opened doors of life in the kingdom to all people. Christianity, like a fairy tale, assured believers of a happy ending and offered them comfort in despair. Hitler, like Jesus, also gave millions of people hope by capturing their imagination.

Is religion really just a spiritual placebo? Shouldn't we be realistic and face life without false hopes? As Judaism, Christianity, and Islam crumble under the impact of change, people will inevitably experience a numbing loss of identity and spiritual despair. Initially, they won't know how to react to the idea that their most deeply held beliefs may be false. Only when all faiths finally realize that they are all flawed will the lost key be found and the door opened again.

Many nonbelievers are convinced that religions are simply hatred machines that divide billions of people and fuel mass atrocities. Millions of people have been tortured, mutilated, and slaughtered in the name of religious morality. Because religion divides all people, instead of uniting them, it is not sacred. The Holy Bible continues to be used to justify extermination and land appropriation. Scripture is the most abused component of religion; its exclusivity will continue to kill us forever.

Religions today tend to neglect the more tolerant, inclusive, and compassionate teachings and, instead, cultivate theologies of hatred, exclusivity, and revenge. For many, the acquisition of artificial religious knowledge (ignorance) creates only confusion and division, which always lead to conflict and tragedy. People are led by a false sense of righteousness (religious indoctrination) to combat the erroneously determined wrong (any differing ideology).

Our attempts at exterminating one another, however, may have more to do with our struggle to survive the evolutionary process than with religion. Religion is merely the weapon of choice. Wars tend to be politically motivated and religiously inspired, a deadly combination.

Common chimpanzees, who share about ninety-eight percent of their genes with humans, wage war. Gangs of neighboring males meet at the borderline of their territories with the express purpose of exterminating their opponents. At the end of the day, it's really about mental, physical, spiritual, and emotional survival.

The kingdom of God is spread upon the earth. The meaning of life is found in our ordinary human existence. Love is the ultimate meaning of life—it is the high point of our being. Love is also a natural human instinct that has absolutely nothing to do with religion. The legacy of religion is contradictory to the concept of love. Jesus commanded us to love one another. Christianity, for the most part, never understood his message.

Personal Truths about Jesus

Jesus was a Jewish mystic and prophet who died as a martyr; he was not a god who died for the sins of humanity (though all things are possible with God, the Bible specifically states that God is immutable and eternal). Jesus was the greatest moral teacher in history. He was an obscure teacher of wisdom, but he was not the Messiah (how can Jesus, a sinless man, be descended from King David, an adulterer and serial-murderer?). Jesus's alternative wisdom and lifestyle generated a boundary-shattering social vision. He believed that tradition and convention were not sacred in themselves.

Jesus stressed love for God and compassion for other people. He served the poor, the lowly, the sick, and the sinner. His spirit of charity, patience, humility, and love of enemies changed the world for the better.

Jesus was a Jewish rabbi who ministered in a unique way; he was able to gather the masses because of his remarkable healing ability. Jesus offered his followers a forgiving God who was the loving Father of all people—rich and poor, Jew and non-Jew.

Jesus demonstrated God's love for all and taught us to embrace God's presence in our lives. The core value of his ethic was compassion, and the heart of his teaching was a commitment to love without boundaries. Jesus's greatest contribution was showing us how to live and to love.

Personal Truths about Christianity

Christianity developed in a time of mysticism and wonder—miracles were commonplace and people were willing to believe the most fantastic stories. The Christian faith was built around Hellenistic mystery religions and a Judeo-Platonic philosophy of God. In retaining many pagan elements in its description of God, Christianity distorted both God and Jesus of Nazareth.

The Christian church thrives on power, control, sin, and guilt. In the past, the church repeatedly tried to kill its enemies and those who threatened its power. Why didn't the church want the Bible translated so that the common person could read it? Was it because of the numerous contradictions contained in the text, or was it about maintaining power and control? The ongoing corruption in the church is an indication of how totally disconnected Christianity is from Jesus.

The church has been so obsessed with increasing its power over its members that it continues to repress doubt and dissent. There is a tendency to stifle individual thought and cultivate conformist mediocrity. Questions challenge institutional security; it is clear that truth is not the primary goal.

Christianity heavily stresses doctrine, theology, and faith. It is a closed system that cannot afford to take alternative views seriously. Guilt, not love, is the fundamental emotion Christianity induces.

Christians are conditioned to place the burden of sorrow on Jesus, as they spin in the neurosis of sin and salvation. They worship his suffering and death instead of celebrating his life and applying his teachings. Most Christians are unaware that they are merely prisoners of religious ideologies and dogmas. In many ways, they are like the people M. Night Shyamalan portrayed in his movie, *The Village*.

Jesus was opposed to institutions—the legacy of Christianity and the church would certainly horrify him. If Jesus were alive today, we would most likely find him conversing with pimps and prostitutes, feeding the poor and homeless, and visiting hospitals, hospices, senior homes, ghettos, and prisons. I doubt that we would find him in a multi-million dollar mega-church filled with thousands of self-righteous hypocrites. Where are we most likely to find you?

Truths That Set Me Free

- Christianity told me that Jesus was God; Jesus taught me that only the Father is God.

- Christianity told me that I was separated from God because of sin; Jesus taught me that the kingdom of God was within me.

- Christianity told me that salvation was based on faith (belief in Jesus's incarnation and resurrection) not works; Jesus taught me that salvation was based on the law, works, and deeds and that faith without deeds is dead. In order to inherit eternal life, Jesus taught that one must follow the law (Mark 10:17–19; Luke 10:25–8*)*.

- Christianity told me to pray en masse and worship Jesus; Jesus taught me to pray in solitude and worship *Our Father.* True worshipers shall worship the Father in spirit and in truth. God is not to be known by reason but by love.

- Christianity is institutional (dogmatic)—Jesus was spiritual (intuitive). Spirituality is a feeling or a state of mind, whereas religion is the result of feelings being codified into law. Religion is nothing more than an attempt to harness innate spirituality for organizational purposes; it tries to express an inexpressible reality. Spirituality gets lost in the laws and rituals of organized religion.

Myth and religion are the human way of understanding and controlling the world, unloading guilt (by washing away sins), and coping with suffering and death. We are the only species on this planet that know we are going to die.

In a spiritual quest for truth, one will never discover what truth is—only what it is not. All previous notions of truth tend to fall away after such a journey. You will only know that you don't know and can't know.

Jesus's teachings are the diamonds buried deep within the "dung" (doctrines, dogmas, and rituals) of Christianity. It is essential that I learn to preach my faith without words.

CHAPTER 3

Building a Faith on Solid Rock

IN MY spiritual quest for God, I climbed the mountains
of world religion, traveled through the deserts of world
history, swam the oceans of world mythology, and navi-
gated the jungles of world philosophy. What I discovered
at the end of my journey is that the one God, God in
the highest, the only God, is the one whom Jesus called
Father. Jesus beautifully revealed this God as the Father
in his parable of the Prodigal Son.

This deity, however, is not the God of Israel or
Islam, nor is it the triune God of Christianity. Jesus
addressed God as "Father" and not as "Yahweh," "Allah,"
or "Trinity." Jesus revealed that another nonviolent,
merciful, and compassionate God exists and that all of
humanity shares this immanent spirit. This God, which
can't be known or named, is the deity in which I believe.

My belief in a Supreme Being stems from a personal revelation and an inner awareness of divinity that is
not to be equated with the "special" revelation of sacred
scripture. It is not my intention to create a God in my
own image or to project my personality into the darkness. I am convinced that the sacred is real.

I am also convinced that God operates on the basis
of free will. Free will and divine intervention are mutu-

ally exclusive. I would like to believe that God is seeking to make all things new and all things one. I would also like to believe that by living in love, we live in God, and God lives in us.

God is a presence in which my being comes alive. And though God's essence always eludes us, he does gradually reveal himself. I take comfort in the idea that God is a holy love that has always been active in creation, offering new revelations and the possibility of eternal life to all people.

God desires the salvation of everyone: all religions can be stairways to heaven. Loving God with all one's heart, mind, soul, and strength and submitting to the divine will are the keys to the gates of heaven. Our ultimate goal should be to combine the love of God with the love of humanity.

I pray (the Lord's Prayer) directly to God in solitude, asking for the strength and wisdom to do his will. I try to deepen my awareness of him through meaningful worship. I yield my life to God, but I also screen what I believe to be his will. Living in a holy relationship with God has become my top priority.

A Spiritual Epiphany

I've always had faith in God, but I was never really sure he existed. A spiritual struggle within my soul, for some unexplainable reason, would not allow me to simply take a leap of faith. This war between belief and unbelief raged in my soul for the first forty years of my life. "Born again" Christianity, at best, was a superficial experience. The comedian Bernie Mac described the extent of my faith when he said, "I don't believe shit until shit happens." It has been said that we shall never believe with a vigorous and unquestioning faith unless God touches our hearts, but we shall believe as soon as he does so.

In the spring of 2002, a Spirit touched my soul in a way that radically transformed my life. God spoke to my heart and convinced me, experientially, that he exists. Revelation is said to be the grace of God because it calls "dead men" to life and sinners to repentance. God's sudden surprise visit touches our lives when we are alone and seeking him out of our joy.

A spiritual epiphany is an unsolicited and moving mystical experience that is difficult to explain. For a brief moment in time, I felt like I was held in a mental state of suspended animation. I didn't see or hear anything. And though I was given no details or direction, I felt like I was asked to do something. Tears ran down my face, but I wasn't sure if they were tears of joy or tears of despair. I wasn't drinking alcohol or using illicit drugs. I wasn't tired and I wasn't hallucinating. All I knew for certain was that God exists and that he wanted me to do something.

I tried to ignore what I believed to be the task: I was supposed to study the sacred scriptures and then write about them. Ironically, the day I convinced myself that I was too busy for God's tasking was the day I lost my job. I felt like Jonah. All of a sudden I had plenty of time to read and write. For years I didn't say anything to anyone because I didn't want people to think I was crazy.

In my personal quest for God, I was amazed at how many similar stories and experiences I encountered (the God gene?). The "religious experience argument" is based on the notion that people have felt the presence of God, have sensed his direction in their lives, and have experienced his strength preparing them for some task. I believe it was Carl Jung who said, "I don't have to believe.

I know!" It is truly a great day when a person can actually say this and mean it. Of course, scientific research into the God gene may eventually prove that my experience of God was simply a figment of my imagination (DNA).

Personal Beliefs about Jesus

Jesus was a divinely inspired prophet; for him, God was an experiential reality. Jesus was seen and heard by people as God's ultimate revelation. His unshakable consciousness of God, unconventional interpretation of Judaism, unsurpassed moral teachings, concern for human suffering, and unequivocal use of "Father" to address God makes him not only unique but holy.

Jesus was a messenger and primary exemplar of God's will. All could practice his way of life: a way of love, service, forgiveness, and prayer. Jesus was a man who helped link human love with divine love.

And though I reject the vast majority of Christian dogma and doctrine, I do believe that Jesus performed healings and that God raised him spiritually from the dead. The significance of Jesus's life and death can transform people's lives. His life and teaching can also mediate consciousness of God in a redemptive and reconciling way.

My hope and wish is that Israel will someday promote Jesus from a false Messiah to one of their greatest prophets and teachers. Similarly, Christians will hopefully demote him from the status of God and will recognize him as simply a prophet of God. I love Jesus, the light that I follow, but I worship only God.

Personal Beliefs about Christianity

Christianity is a faith that wants you to believe that an immutable and eternal God died. Blind faith is obviously a prerequisite. Christianity got both God and Jesus of Nazareth very badly wrong. Nothing between Jesus's birth and death appears to be essential to his mission or to the faith of the church. The Christ of faith undermines many of Jesus's intentions and teachings. Historically, organized Christianity has been a great mistake. For many, it's the greatest misfortune of humanity.

Contemporary Christianity needs to make a radical break with its past. In order to maintain some semblance of credibility in the future, Christianity will have to discard most of its doctrines, relinquish its exclusive claims to truth, and abandon the belief that it is the only true path to God. Jesus's moral teachings are really the heart of Christianity; doctrines are relatively unimportant.

Jesus's preaching concerning God was inclusive and universal in scope. Replacing exclusive Christianity with a truly universal religion of love should be Christianity's ultimate goal. A sense of peace, serenity, and loving-kindness are the hallmarks of all true religious insight. The world desperately needs a universal faith of timeless truths that embraces all of humanity.

Truth and Wisdom

Reconstructing theological beliefs is a personal responsibility. Over the years, I've had to work extremely hard to put my confusion on these issues in order. As a matter of fact, it nearly drove me insane just trying to separate fact from fiction. I am not convinced that I am anywhere near getting anything right.

People have to fight for truth—greatness of soul is required for such an endeavor. A person must be severe with his or her heart. One must question everything and expose the lies. The key is to find a truth that is true for you—an idea for which you can live and die. Real truth is not a matter of detached, abstract speculation or doctrine; it is a matter of painful heart-searching.

Is there anything that is truly sacred or holy? Religions that divide humanity are not sacred. Each religion believes in something extraordinary, romantic, and unrealistic. Religion also pretends to conceive the immeasurable, the timeless, the transcendent; it projects all kinds of illusory images.

Human beings long for certainty. The reality, however, is that there is no real psychological security in human religions. There is no security, physical or psychological, whatsoever; nothing in life or death is guaranteed.

Philosopher J. Krishnamurti said that most of us are caught in some kind of illusion: the illusion of being or not being, the illusion of power or status. He also said that a mind that is caught in illusion has no order. Strong belief in something that happened thousands of years ago, doesn't confirm the reality of the event. Many people speak from illusions that have resulted from religious indoctrination. Totally unaware, humans not only deceive others, but themselves. This is the problem with faith. We need to learn how to stop confusing facts with faith and passion with evidence.

Are we simply cowards who are afraid of death? In our longing for God, heaven, and security, did we imprison ourselves within ideology and illusion? Are we merely slaves to habit, tradition, and conformity? Why do we cling to the misery that we already know instead of searching for truth? Why must we continue to suffer in a

universal sorrow of ignorance? The undeveloped humanity, living not in terms of itself but in terms of an imposed
system, is the threat that we all face today.

According to J. Krishnamurti, one must be free of
all ideologies. Ideologies are dangerous illusions. Every
form of ideology—political, philosophical, religious,
social, or personal—ends up in religious conditioning.
To live without comparison is to remove a tremendous
burden; one must be free of all conclusions.

John P. Meier said, "The historical Jesus subverts
not just some ideologies but all ideologies." The moment
a person ceases to confuse the self with the useless ideologies (myths, superstitions, religions) created by others,
the mind will be liberated. We must, however, keep in
mind that man does not live by bread alone. Learn to live
as a human being by holding to your own ideals and by
rejecting the system's impersonal claims upon you.

Persons pursuing the study of ultimate truth will
never find it. Ultimate truth cannot be put into words
or images. That which is measurable can never find the
immeasurable, which is truth. As you continue to seek
the immeasurable, however, it may find you.

What is the source of life and what happens after
death? No one knows. Other than decomposition, we
have no actual knowledge of what takes place after death.
The only thing we really have is our beliefs, and we can
never be completely sure that our beliefs correspond to
reality. Unfortunately, what we believe is often either in-
defensible or contradictory.

The mystery of life and eternity is beyond all human conception. The whole struggle in the world, both
physiological and psychological, is to find security and
permanency. However, we neither know nor control
what comes to be. The fairy tales we create to give our-

selves comfort and security make us misfits in reality. Our truths are merely those illusions without which we cannot live. Ultimate truth can only be determined in actual death; near-death experiences don't count.

Fuse eternity with the present. The kingdom of God is spread upon the earth: realize it and try to see it. You do not control your life; you have to learn to give up what you never really had and get out of your own way. Devote your heart and soul to seeking the Lord your God. Those who search for truth out of their joy achieve a state of grace. God, in his own time, chooses to connect with those who are a part of him.

Wisdom is following your bliss: align your life with your soul. Wisdom knows that love is the most powerful force in the universe and that compassion is the highest form of intelligence. Jesus's wisdom teaching calls us to a life centered not on religious tradition, institution, or convention, but on love and compassion.

Joy is not in hoarding but in giving. Be open to everything and attached to nothing. A liberated person is said to walk away from the snares of the world. Joyfully participate in the fragmentation of life and work without abandon in the midst of the suffering and sorrows of this world. Embrace the messiness of life. Overcome the love of power with the power of love, and you will find peace. The good life is one inspired by love and guided by knowledge, devotion, and selfless action.

At the End of the Day

I am a follower of Jesus of Nazareth. Jesus does not have to be God for my faith to have meaning and validity. Other than God, Jesus of Nazareth has been the most influential person in my life. Religion plays no role in what I choose to believe. I have "a knowing" of God and I follow the life and teachings of Jesus.

I no longer have faith in faith; I no longer have hope in hope; but I have faith and hope in love. Jesus gave only one commandment, and that was love; it brings us near to God and to one another.

I began this quest with an epiphany—a "knowing" of God. I no longer feel a need to live by faith. My experience of God sent me on a five-year journey that constantly chipped away at my soul. I realize that seeking God and pursuing spiritual truth is an ongoing process, and yet I feel blessed with what I've discovered thus far.

At the end of the day, I was able to find a spiritual guide—a light for the path to God. I found Jesus. I found the clear and undistorted son who was especially loved by God.

Epilogue

I AM interested in truth and not in faith. Truth has one reality whereas faith has infinite interpretations. Jesus said that we would know the truth and that the truth would set us free. So what is truth and how does it set us free?

The truth is that all religions are false. Knowing this truth can free us from institutions and ideologies that indoctrinate, divide, bind, steal, and kill. In a time of universal deceit, even the most brainwashed individual can find liberation.

We can still choose to believe in a God and an after-life that may or may not exist. Socrates said, "I only know that I don't know anything." This statement, this truth, is really the only answer to all our great questions. As for those who claim to know everything, they're killing us.